D0862193

How To Keep Your Child Out of Special Education

Ann Core Greenberg Ph.D.

FINKELSTEIN
MEMORIAL LIBRARY
SPRING VALLEY, NY

3 2191 00927 4795

How to Keep Your Child Out of Special Education

First published in 2010 by Ecademy Press
48 St Vincent Drive, St Albans, Herts, AL1 5SJ
info@ecademy-press.com
www.ecademy-press.com

Printed and Bound by Lightning Source in the UK and USA

Set in Helvetica Neue by Emma Lewis

Printed on acid-free paper from managed forests.
This book is printed on demand, so no copies will be
remaindered or pulped.

ISBN 978-1-905823-76-5

The right of Ann Greenberg to be identified as the
author of this work has been asserted in accordance with
sections 77 and 78 of the Copyright Designs and Patents
Act 1988.

A CIP catalogue record for this book is available from the
British Library.

All rights reserved. No part of this work may be reproduced
in any material form (including photocopying or storing in any
medium by electronic means and whether or not transiently
or incidentally to some other use of this publication) without
the written permission of the copyright holder except in
accordance with the provisions of the Copyright, Designs
and Patents Act 1988. Applications for the Copyright holder's
written permission to reproduce any part of this publication
should be addressed to the publishers.

Copyright © 2010 Ann Greenberg

In memory of my father

Notice to Readers

Names of children described in this book were changed to protect their privacy. Children described may be composites of several children or fictional for illustrative purposes.

Acknowledgements

This book has been brewing in my mind for fifteen years as I worked with many parents who shared their worries with me. Parents repeatedly stated that they wanted to help their children do better in school but did not know what they could do to help. They often said they wanted their children to get past whatever was blocking their progress and to succeed in school. Although parents were often aware of how helpful special education services are for many students, they hoped their children would be able to work satisfactorily within regular education.

I would like to thank all the parents and students with whom I worked for their support and trust as we have worked together. I would like to thank all the psychologists and teachers with whom I have worked for their numerous consultations and suggestions for students that over the years helped me hone the information and guidance presented in this book. There were many wonderful colleagues but special appreciation goes to Mrs. Fayga Ringel, Mrs. Rena Rosenblum, Dr. Kawana Reed-Perricone, Dr. Beatrice Alpert, Dr. Morton Frank, Mr. Dennis Feinstein, and Mr. James Hughes.

Thanks also go to Mindy Gibbins-Klein who helped me take my inspiration and shape it into an actual book. Thanks to Fern Spinazzola and Eileen Wilkinson for their comments on the manuscript from a parent's perspective.

Last but not least, I thank my family for their encouragement and support throughout the process of producing this book.

CONTENTS

INTRODUCTION

What this book is about

How would you like to spend thirteen years at a job where you feel confused and inadequate, struggle to please the boss, and worry what your co-workers think about you and your performance? Doesn't sound so good, yet that is the scenario for many school children from kindergarten to twelfth grade. There are nearly seven million special education students in the United States and over $12 billion of federal money is spent on special education services each year. There are children who must receive special education services in order to progress academically. There are also children at risk of needing special education services who may be able to remain in regular education with appropriate support from home, community, and school. These are the children within the scope of this book. The intent of *How To Keep Your Child Out Of Special Education* is to inform, support, and empower parents to obtain appropriate educational support for their academically struggling children, with the goal of avoiding special education services.

As a parent, you want your child to have a successful school experience. You want your son, your daughter, to learn the curriculum, to develop warm, lasting friendships, and to be prepared to manage in the world upon graduation, regardless of the subsequent endeavors he or she may pursue. If your child needs help succeeding in school, you want to get it, but you would prefer to avoid labels that might be stigmatizing or embarrassing. You worry that once a child is classified as a special education student, it may be hard for him or her to return to a regular education program. This worry is understandable as many (but certainly not all) classified children maintain their classified status throughout their school years. You want to help your child regain his academic footing using non-special education supports but are not sure how to go about it. This book aims to inform and support your efforts.

Why I wrote this book

I have a Ph.D. in Clinical Psychology, and am licensed as a Clinical Psychologist and certified as a School Psychologist. Over the past twenty-five years, I have worked in hospital, clinic, college and private practice settings, as well as in schools. I have been a School Psychologist for fifteen years, interacting with children from a wide variety of socio-economic, religious, racial, and ethnic backgrounds. I wrote this book because I have had numerous parents approach me, worried about their children but not aware of what they could do to help them. Parents are far more powerful than they usually give themselves credit for. They just don't always know what resources are available or how to go about getting them for their children. Sometimes they are not aware of resources because they are accustomed to private schools that may have offered less than public schools, sometimes because they did not grow up in the United States, and sometimes, probably most frighteningly for them, because they never needed to know about academic support services before now.

There are also times when I see that parents worry for nothing. Their expectations for their child are off the mark, inappropriate for the child's age, grade, or developmental level. A child might have performed poorly on one test, leading parents to jump to negative conclusions, when in fact the child is performing fine overall. Your own school history, whether positive or negative, can also distort your perception of how your child is doing.

Every day at work I see students learning, growing, and benefiting from special education services. I have no doubt that special education services do a lot of good for many students and that many students cannot progress without them. However, based on what plenty of parents and students tell me, I also have no doubt that they would prefer not to need special education services. Students with milder forms of learning challenge may be able to avoid special education if they take advantage of supports available at home, at school, and in the community. This requires much effort and determination, patience and perseverance, from both students and parents.

I am one of those who believe it is worth the effort. Both as an educator and as a parent, I believe that one should make every effort and pursue all avenues that may help one's child to regain his or her academic equilibrium. This is true whether the child is at risk of needing special education or temporarily facing a particular academic challenge. I addressed this myself with my daughters. I paid for speech therapy in the community for one daughter and got up extra early in the morning to take the other to school for tutoring when it was necessary. It wasn't fun but it was important for my children's well-being.

A case at work

Dana is a six–year–old first grade student, whose mother and teacher worry about her classroom functioning. Her teachers describe her as bright, friendly, and eager to succeed in school. They also note her difficulty with fine motor skills, especially writing. The pencil always seems to fall out of her hand, her letters appear at angles to the line, and although Dana is willing to persevere, it takes her a long time to finish writing her sentences. Dana's best friend is a special education student who receives Occupational Therapy among other services, so Dana's parents are aware that services are possible. Dana's mother believes her daughter needs some help but doubts that her child's needs are significant enough to qualify her for special education services. Besides, she does not want Dana to be classified, just helped. Dana's mother consults with an Occupational Therapist in private practice in her community. The therapist works with Dana after school to develop her fine motor skills. She teaches her how to hold a pencil correctly, gives strategies for producing stable letters, and encourages Dana to learn to type. In addition, Dana's mother brings her to school thirty minutes early every day so that Dana can meet with her teacher and get extra writing practice time. As a result, Dana is making steady progress. Her pencil stays in her hand and her letters no longer dance on the line. She can write faster and her typing skills make her feel very grown up. Although Dana's mother has to pay a fee for the therapy and get Dana to school extra early, she is satisfied because Dana does not miss class time for therapy, her confidence is high, and best of all Dana is performing satisfactorily. Mother is delighted to see that her efforts to obtain help for Dana within regular education and the community are working out. She is pleased that Dana is progressing appropriately without special education services.

Dana's mother found a way to address her daughter's needs within regular education. This book will support you in your search for and among options to address your child's academic needs.

How to use this book

How To Keep Your Child Out of Special Education is not a comprehensive text nor is it an explanation of resources in a particular school district or community. Rather, it is a general guide for you, the parent, to help you find out what types of academic support are available to your child in the community and in your child's school, regardless of whether it is public or private, religious or non-sectarian, traditional or non-traditional. It is also a guide to the enormously important contributions that you can make at home.

Each chapter ends with a summary of the key points and a list of questions for you to consider, in order to help you develop and focus on a plan of action that is right for your child. Chapters address the issues of understanding your child's current academic situation, misconceptions that you might have, your feelings and your child's feelings regarding his or her academic issues, support strategies in the home, time management and use of community resources, and various non-special education academic supports available in school. Guidance is also provided should you decide that it would be advisable to inquire regarding special education services. This book is based on the premise that you expect your child to apply himself in school and that you are ready to apply yourself to supporting his efforts. Turn the page, and together we will strive to understand and address your child's academic needs.

CHAPTER ONE

YOUR CHILD FINDS IT HARD TO LEARN

Why are you concerned about how your child is performing in school? What makes you think he or she is not doing okay?

As parents we want to see our children learn and progress appropriately in school. It is painful to watch a child struggle to grasp concepts and skills, confused and frustrated day after day. Homework becomes a tearful torment not only for the child but for the entire family. So many children sail through school smoothly; why is my child having difficulties? What can I do to help? As a psychologist employed by a public school district, I frequently encounter parents struggling with these questions. Together we can work to find answers for your child.

The purpose of this book is to help parents of children (primarily, but not exclusively, elementary school children) who are having difficulty keeping up academically. These children have mild to moderate   difficulty learning their curriculum. Such children may have poor study habits, some fine motor weakness, or mild difficulty with speech or language. They are within normal limits cognitively, some possibly toward the lower end of normal intelligence. The children have difficulty organizing their work and study materials. They are inconsistently effective in their role as students although they are well behaved and respectful of adult authority. Despite the above weaknesses, these children have four key strengths. They behave appropriately, care how they do in school, are motivated, and want to succeed.

You, the parent, are worried. You want to help your child get back on track and perform satisfactorily in school but are not sure how. You are aware that special education services exist but strongly prefer that your child not become classified as a special education student if at all possible.

There are several reasons to avoid special education services if a student can be satisfactorily supported otherwise. To the extent possible, children should be educated in mainstream classes with typically developing peers. This permits exposure to a standard curriculum and interaction with other children of age-appropriate mental, physical, social, and emotional development. Many parents and children feel that a stigma is attached to special education. Children may think they are "stupid," and often feel social as well as academic embarrassment. Likewise, parents often feel embarrassed when their children's difficulties become "official." They want the academic help but not the "label."

Parents are also concerned about special education services because classified students as a group have a lower rate of graduation from high school, or may graduate with a special education diploma rather than with a standard diploma or a diploma that reflects higher educational achievement (e.g., Regents, International Baccalaureate). This in turn may affect the student's ability to obtain employment or enroll in further studies.

Special education is also time consuming as parents need to spend more time consulting with teachers, psychologists, and other special education staff, completing paperwork, and attending meetings. Special education is expensive for school districts (and ultimately for parents as taxpayers) in terms of time, manpower, and testing materials. Approximately $12 billion of federal money is spent on special education in the United States each year. Given that there are nearly seven million special education students in the United States, there are many children at risk.

The title of the book notwithstanding, special education is not a place but a service, which some children must have in order to make academic progress. This book is not intended for students who have mental retardation, autism, severe emotional disability, traumatic brain injury, or are in any other way significantly impaired. This book aims to help those students who have mild to moderate academic difficulties to perform satisfactorily in school, so that they may be maintained in regular education and not require special education services.

What do you expect your child to know at his or her grade level?

It is possible that your child is progressing appropriately and that you are worrying for nothing. Sometimes parents misunderstand or are unclear about what is expected at a specific grade level. This can be easily addressed by speaking with the teacher, principal or curriculum director. There are books available in libraries and bookstores that describe the typical curricula for each grade level although it is to be expected that there will be differences in how curricula are approached and presented by different schools or districts. You may be worried that your first grade daughter does not know multiplication and division, when these subjects are typically introduced in third or fourth grade. Clearing up a misunderstanding can bring relief that the child is in fact progressing at a grade-expected level.

What is your definition of "satisfactory school performance?"

It is also possible that you have a different definition of "satisfactory school performance" than the definition held by your child's teacher. Many parents, especially those who were scholastically successful themselves, define "satisfactory school performance" as earning a straight A average. Public school districts tend to define "satisfactory school performance" as a C average. The student is producing average, age-typical level work, consistent with standards for passing the class. While producing above average work is desirable, it is not necessary for a definition of "satisfactory." Not every student can be an A student. To expect consistent A's is unrealistic pressure on a student; to expect consistent strong effort is appropriate.

Sometimes, a private school may expect students to earn A's and B's, while C's are considered equivalent to a failure. That the parents are paying tuition can sometimes lead to an expectation that Junior will get good marks. Some private school teachers told me that their school administrator discourages them from putting poor grades on the report cards because the tuition paying parents won't like it. The grades may also represent effort or behavior combined with actual performance, which muddies the picture. Such "courtesy" report cards, as I call them, are misleading. I have seen many private school report cards where the grades themselves are good but the accompanying comments are less so. This duality can mislead parents into thinking their child is working at a higher level than is in fact the case, because they will be inclined to believe the good grade. This sets the stage for trouble later on, when the student fails to keep up and the teacher clearly criticizes the student's performance. I believe in "truth in advertising" report cards, with separate grades for behavior, effort, and performance. Polite, kind classroom behavior is highly desirable but does not compensate for poor reading comprehension. You can average the results of several quizzes but you cannot average together good behavior and poor division skills.

Academics is not a competitive sport

Sometimes parents worry when they hear how well another child does. Just because Bruce is advanced in arithmetic does not mean that Larry isn't doing just fine. There are parents who brag, exaggerate, and just plain show off. Let them enjoy themselves. Even if their child really is a genius, it is not a criticism of your child. Your son or daughter is a unique person with his or her own personality, strengths, challenges, interests and outlook on life.

Get the facts about your child's performance

How do you go about getting the facts? Start by gathering your child's report cards, homework sheets, and classroom work. Read them very carefully. Then read the teacher's comments very carefully. Go past the polite, encouraging remarks and look for the meat of the comments. What comes up? Does Russell do fine on rote tasks but struggle with inferential thinking? Does Jane use the vocabulary words taught in class or rely on simpler words or word substitutes such as "thing," "it," or "that?" Does your child participate in class? Does he ask questions or make connections to previous lessons or life experiences? Is there a pattern to the teacher's comments? Do you see a good mark but comments that seem to undermine it? For example, the comment accompanying Jonah's fourth grade report card that contained mostly A's and B's was "Jonah has great capabilities. With more effort and enthusiasm, his capabilities will come to fruition." This comment suggests that the teacher thinks "fruition" has not in fact happened yet, despite writing good marks on the report card that suggest it did.

Meet with your child's classroom teacher. The teacher works with twenty-five or so students in the class and has seen hundreds over the years, giving him or her a broad perspective and basis of comparison. Ask the teacher to describe and discuss how your child is doing. Review the report cards and work assignments with her.

Some questions to ask:

1. Does my child seem happy at school? Does he display a positive attitude?
2. Does he follow classroom routines?
3. Does he participate in class? Raise his hand to volunteer, ask questions, seek clarification?
4. Does she work appropriately in pairs or groups?
5. Does she hand in her homework punctually?
6. Does she need frequent assistance? Seem confused? Grasp directions easily?
7. Is he using information posted in the class-room to help himself?
8. Is his work orderly, legible, clean?
9. Are his comments logical and relevant?
10. Does he have friends, do the other children include him in play, want to work with him?
11. Is he making appropriate academic progress for his age/grade?
12. Where does she rank in the class compared to her peers?
13. Is promotion in doubt?
14. Does the teacher have any concerns not raised above?

Listen carefully and take notes. Both parents should review the child's work and both should attend the meeting with the teacher if possible. Are the teacher's concerns new this year or consistent with what last year's teacher said? What has the teacher been doing to support your child? What has been helpful? What strategies did not help? What have you tried at home to help your child that you could share with the teacher? What are the teacher's suggestions going forward?

To understand how your child's work compares to that of his classmates, ask to see the work of your child's peers, some of which may be posted on a hallway bulletin board or on the classroom walls. Request that the teacher show you work that is average, typical work, as well as samples of excellent work. (Students' names can be removed or covered if necessary.) People tend to think "average" is undesirable, but this misses the point. By definition, most people are average in whatever you measure, e.g., height, weight, running speed, IQ, etc. Average is normal and expected. It is unrealistic to compare yourself to a star and conclude that you are a failure. Of course you don't play basketball as skillfully as Michael Jordan or the cello as beautifully as Yo-Yo Ma. It's not a fair comparison—they are experts in their fields. Rather, ask do you play basketball well enough so you enjoy playing with your friends? When you play the cello do you hear music or squeaks? Are you making progress as you practice? Likewise, it is unfair to expect your child to produce perfect schoolwork. It is fair to expect him to put forth his best effort and to make progress over time. It is fair to be concerned if despite true consistent effort, your child's work falls below the level expected of a student in his grade.

Don't forget to speak with the key player, your child. How does he feel about school and his work? Is your son worried, willing, frightened, eager, or avoidant? Does your daughter look forward to school or moan and groan? Not every child, especially young ones, can or will speak of their feelings, but you will get a pretty good idea how your child thinks he or she is performing academically whether the response is verbal or nonverbal.

Signs that you should be concerned

In your review of grades and teacher's comments on report cards and assignments, do you see a pattern? Are the same comments coming up year after year or across subject areas from different teachers? Consider a comment such as "Jacob is a friendly, kind boy who is well behaved. He often needs encouragement and repetition of directions but works willingly on assigned tasks." On the surface, it seems like praise and some of it is. Jacob tries to do his work and his behavior is fine. What's not so fine is that Jacob needs to repeat and process the directions more slowly than his peers do. He is reluctant to begin working without extra support from the teacher.

At home, Jacob follows a routine to start his homework. He goes to his desk and sharpens his pencil, lines up his ruler and eraser, and opens his workbook to the correct page. He reads the first question. Then Jacob gets stuck and slows down. He looks out of the window, down at his book, and out of the window again. He tries to answer the first question but is not sure that his answer is right. He asks Mommy for help. Mommy helps him read the directions and asks Jacob what he thinks he is supposed to do. Jacob appears confused. Mommy asks if Jacob has a similar question in his notebook that he could look at. By reading the question in his notebook and with Mommy's gentle guidance, Jacob thinks some more and writes an answer to the first question.

Meanwhile, Jacob's baby sister cries and Mommy needs to change her diaper. Jacob tries the second question, not sure he understands all the words. Eventually, Jacob starts crying that the homework is too hard and that he can't do it by himself. Mommy would like to help Jacob more but she has to take care of the baby, fold laundry, and prepare dinner. Mommy is worried that Jacob struggles so often with his homework. She believes that children ought to be able to complete their homework on their own or mostly on their own. It should not be so hard for Jacob to do.

When Mommy visited Jacob's school on Parents' Night, she looked at Jacob's work hanging on the class bulletin board. She also looked at the work of the other children in Jacob's class. A number of children seemed to produce work that was more detailed and contained bigger vocabulary words. Not all of the other children did so, but enough to make Mommy wonder. While reading the work on the bulletin board, Mommy considered that recently Jacob spoke against school: "I don't want to go to school today. I want to stay home with you, Mommy." He also seemed to have a lot of stomach aches lately, although never on weekends and holidays. Mommy knew she had to do something to help Jacob. He had a lot more years of school ahead of him and he had to be able to get through them satisfactorily, for his own sake and for that of the whole family.

Should I speak to someone?

In their conversation, Jacob's teacher discussed with Mommy what she had tried in the classroom to help Jacob, and considered which strategies worked and which had not. The teacher reminded Jacob to use information posted on the classroom walls, such as posters depicting the values of various coins, maps of the United States, and the vocabulary words of the week. This strategy was successful in that Jacob willingly checked the posters when reminded but unsuccessful in that he did not consistently check the posters without being reminded, nor did he always grasp how the information was relevant to his task.

Mommy recalled that her neighbor's daughter had had some difficulty in school but had been able to overcome it. Mommy spoke with the neighbor and asked how she had handled the problem. The neighbor recommended that Mommy consult the school's psychologist. At first Mommy was nervous to do so but the neighbor explained that the psychologist meets with families all the time. "A lot of your worries about talking to a psychologist are misconceptions and wrong information; I know mine were. Don't be afraid. The psychologist will show you many things you can do to help Jacob. We got lots of good advice and our Sarah is doing just fine now."

What do School Psychologists do?

School Psychologists provide a wide range of services to assist students at school. These services include consultations with teachers, administrators, and parents, direct counseling with students, assessment of students' cognitive, behavioral, and emotional functioning, and crisis intervention. School Psychologists develop intervention plans and recommend appropriate remedial, supportive, or special educational services to improve students' academic, behavioral, or social functioning. They also help parents and teachers connect to community resources that may be beneficial to students. School Psychologists also share their professional knowledge via classroom visits, informational assemblies, Parent-Teacher Association meetings, and staff development workshops.

Sharing your concerns with the School Psychologist

Call the School Psychologist for an appointment and explain the reason for the meeting so that the psychologist can schedule a time to address your concerns. Coming in unannounced can backfire as the psychologist might be meeting with another parent or working with a student. State your child's full legal name as listed in school records, his date of birth, grade and teacher so the psychologist can observe him in class and read previous report cards and other available records. This preparation will enable the psychologist to start getting to know your child and have a picture of him or her as you speak. In the meeting, share your concerns, your observations of your child at home, his comments regarding schoolwork, and any special issues your child may have (e.g., English as a second language, mild vision impairment, shyness with peers, etc.).

The psychologist will discuss with you the strengths and weaknesses you perceive in your child. Together you will work to pinpoint where the academic concerns lie (for example, subtraction with regrouping or drawing inferences from a text). The psychologist will discuss with you the options available to you to help your child. Some of those options are carried out at home, some involve your working with community resources, and some are available within the school.

Many parents wonder if their child needs to be tested. They are worried that their child might require special education. These worries tend to arise because they are not aware of all the other things that can be done to help children. Sometimes friends or teachers jump the gun and talk about testing, special education or both. Testing, in and of itself, does not do anything to fix your child's problem. Testing is not necessarily relevant to the situation. There's an old saying, "if your only tool is a hammer, all your problems look like nails."

Sometimes, parents request testing because they are unaware of other options, but sometimes it is because they do not understand what it means to test a student. Mrs. Jones may simply want reassurance that little Junior is performing as well as his peers. She may not understand that the school district tests to determine if Junior is a disabled student as defined by law. If Mrs. Jones has no intention of permitting Junior to be enrolled in a special education program or service, she is making an inappropriate request. Likewise, if Mrs. Jones does not believe that Junior is disabled, requesting testing is the wrong avenue to pursue. Testing requires that the student miss several hours of classroom instruction. It requires many hours of staff time and expensive materials. If parents request testing, it should be because they truly believe their child may be a handicapped student in need of special education services. Testing is not the way to check how Junior is doing in class. It should not be requested out of parental curiosity just to see how smart Junior is (you may be disappointed). Testing is a complex, time-consuming process with significant consequences; it should only be pursued when there is a serious concern that a child may meet the legal definition of an educationally handicapped student.

Many problems can be addressed without testing; sometimes you just need a little creativity. For example, Bobby, a third grader, found it hard to start his school day following third grade routines and declined to enter the classroom. This could have developed into a complicated case of school refusal or Bobby could have been tested unnecessarily. Knowing Bobby's IQ and academic functioning were irrelevant as he gave little concern regarding academics. Instead, Bobby's teacher arranged for him to spend the first thirty minutes of the day in his brother's kindergarten class. Having seventeen little kids look up to him as the big, powerful third grader boosted Bobby's self-regard and confidence. This creative, easy to implement solution enabled Bobby to integrate peacefully into his third grade room and have a pleasant day.

Depending on how a problem plays out, testing may become a later step, but it is never the first step because it is not necessarily relevant and may not be able to provide an answer to the particular question or concern. Psychologists and other school staff seek solutions relevant to the problem. We would prefer to find a solution that is appropriate and practical and that helps the student to help himself. Should testing become appropriate, we will explain why. If special education appears needed, we will discuss it. Meanwhile, we strive to support your child in regular education and to facilitate his or her development of needed academic skills.

Response to Intervention

The various forms of help a child may receive at home, in the community, and in school are interventions. Some examples of interventions are one-to-one teaching, small group remediation classes, differentiated instruction or accommodations in the classroom. It is hoped that the appropriate intervention will be determined and employed successfully to enable the child to function satisfactorily in the regular education classroom. Even if a child's academic difficulties are such that parents believe the student will require special education, part of the determination of a student's qualification for special education services is the demonstration that reasonable intervention(s) has been tried for a reasonable period of time and has not proved sufficient. "Response to intervention" or "RTI" is thus important, either because it may resolve the child's academic difficulties or provide support for the need for special education services. While RTI usually refers to interventions that occur in school, it is possible for a home- or community-based intervention to be what the child needs. There are many forms that intervention and support for your struggling student can take. These will be addressed in greater detail in Chapters Five, Six, and Seven.

When a child has difficulty in school, it is natural for a parent to worry and wonder what to do. You can best help your child by getting the facts on his or her academic performance and educating yourself as to available sources of help. The goal is to support your child so that he or she can be successfully maintained in regular education.

Key points from Chapter One:

1. You are worried about your child's academic performance. Do you need to be?
2. Find out how your child is doing. Review grades and teacher's comments on report cards and assignments. Compare your child's work to that of peers. Consult with teacher.
3. You should be concerned if you see the same teacher concerns repeatedly, your child's work seems weaker than that of peers, your child is unhappy about school or appears to be acting out with poor behavior or dubious illnesses.
4. Consult with the School Psychologist. Discuss your options for helping your child. Options exist at home, in the community, and in school. There are many options that can support your child in regular education.
5. Do not automatically request testing. Testing may not mean what you think it means, and may be irrelevant.

Questions for parents to pursue:

1. What are the facts about my child's academic functioning?
2. What are my child's feelings about his or her academic performance?
3. What are my feelings about my child's academic performance?
4. What can I do to support my child's academic functioning?

CHAPTER TWO

YOUR CHILD WANTS TO SUCCEED IN SCHOOL BUT DOESN'T KNOW HOW

The parent-teacher meeting

"Timmy performs satisfactorily in math," began Ms. Breen as she opened the third grade parent-teacher conference. "He's got his math facts pretty solidly and knows some of the times tables by heart. But reading, Mrs. White, that's Tim's challenge. He decodes just fine, but he has trouble grasping deeper meaning in the text."

"What doesn't he understand?" worried Tim's mother.

"Tim finds it hard to draw inferences from contextual language. He doesn't predict possible outcomes in stories," replied the teacher.

"Give me an example, please" said Mrs. White.

"Yesterday we read a story about a boy who needs to wear glasses. In the story, the boy bumps into things and confuses what he sees. Tim understood the fact that the boy had poor vision without his glasses. He didn't understand the boy's dilemma that he couldn't see properly without glasses but was upset about having to wear them."

"How did you know that?" asked Tim's mother.

"Tim knows what glasses are for," replied Ms. Breen. "He understood that the boy bumped into things because he couldn't see well. But in the story, the boy puts on his glasses, looks in the mirror, and is *dismayed to see his owlish face*. Tim couldn't draw the inference that the boy was unhappy about how he looked wearing the glasses. He didn't know vocabulary such as "dismayed." He didn't connect that "owlish" is not a compliment. So he didn't get the boy's frustration at being dependent on something that made him feel ugly. Tim needs to increase his vocabulary and improve his understanding of how language provides meaning."

Why is Tim struggling? What is hindering him from increasing his vocabulary and using language clues to determine the meaning of what he reads? Does he have poor study skills? Surely he has strong feelings about his difficulty with reading. Is he advocating for himself? Is he afraid of what peers might think? Is he worried what his parents will think or do?

Your child may have poor study skills

"How could I have failed the spelling test? I read the list of words ten times!" "I read the chapter twice and I still don't get it." Sound familiar? Many children are willing to work hard, put in plenty of effort, but in fact are just "spinning their wheels" because they are not studying in effective, useful ways.

I have had conversations about studying with numerous students and am amazed at how few of them have received, or recall receiving, formal instruction in how to study and take tests. I do not recall such lessons from my own school days either. "A few teachers gave us tips here and there but no real lessons about studying or taking tests" was the most common answer. When study skills were taught, it was usually in the context of test preparation, remedial instruction or private tutoring, but not during standard class time. My informal conversations with students do not represent a statistical research sample, but nonetheless raise concerns that many students are not given clear, organized instruction in the basic foundation skills of their "job." Teachers rehearse fire drill procedures and parents teach children how to steer and balance a bicycle, yet somehow children are expected to just know how to study. Children know they need to work hard in studying but they often misunderstand what working hard means. They need to know how to work hard *effectively*.

Children's questions reveal areas that require further instruction. "How can I take notes and listen at the same time? I try but then I don't understand my notes." This is a very good question that likely means the child needs to learn what taking notes is and is not. "I read the chapter three times and still don't get it" suggests that the student does not know how to read a textbook versus a storybook. "But I studied all night!" righteously complains a student, who therefore did not get a good night's sleep and was too groggy to concentrate during the test.

There are also students who disparage their abilities or display self-defeating behavior. Is homework a battle in your house because Suzie puts off doing it until Sunday evening? Does she try to do it on the school bus in the morning? "Oh Mom, the teacher never checks it anyway." Of course the teacher will check the homework the day Suzie did not do it. Even if the teacher does not catch her, who is Suzie hurting? Herself. She is hurting her own learning. The teacher already knows long division.

"But I just don't test well. No matter how much I study I still don't test well." There are test taking techniques that can be learned as well as relaxation techniques to help a student "pull himself together" if he starts getting anxious during an exam. These techniques can be helpful to all students, not just those with learning weaknesses. Such strategies will be discussed further in Chapters Six and Seven.

Children have strong feelings about academics and themselves

The statements voiced above can lead to negative feelings not just about school work but about the child himself. "I'm always confused; I never know how to start. When the teacher helps me start, I never know what to do after she goes to help another kid," says Sarah Jane. So what does Sarah Jane do? She sits there, fiddles with her pencil, sometimes asks another kid for help, but usually does nothing. She feels she can't, that she's helpless. She needs specific skills, as well as encouragement and repetitious practice, in order to progress so she can overcome her self-perception as helpless. She learned to feel helpless but the good news is that she can unlearn it.

Another frequently heard comment is "I'm stupid. Everybody else gets it, everybody else knows what to do and I never do." When you are struggling to learn something and you see that someone else grasps it, there can be a tendency to think that there is something wrong with you. This feeling can be intensified if several other people are "getting it" and you are not. As one fifth grader said to me, "they can call it the green group, the robins, or group four; it's still the dummy reading group and everybody knows it." Actually, that's true. Everyone in the class does know which reading group is the best, the second best, the third level and the lowest. What the struggling reader does not realize is that the other children are too busy thinking about themselves to think about which group he's in.

Effective studying is studying that enables a student to understand and remember information and to apply it appropriately in relevant contexts. Teachers can help students by explaining how the information taught in the classroom will be useful to them in their lives. Effective studying involves in-classroom techniques as well as at-home strategies. While there is not just one right way to study, there are established strategies that can be taught, learned and utilized as appropriate in different academic situations.

"I'm allergic to school."

Are you and the school nurse on a first name basis now? Is Reuben a "frequent flyer" to her office? How many times does Reuben need a band aid, an ice pack, have a headache, etc.? Does he try to leave school early? Does Reuben often wake up with a stomach ache, headache, or other mysterious illness on school days? Funny how he never gets a stomach ache when there is a field trip, a special assembly, or sports day at school. Some parents told me that once they are sure there really isn't anything medically wrong with their child, they call his bluff by having him miss something he wants to attend. ("Oh Johnny, you had a stomach ache yesterday. I sure wouldn't want you to throw up on the bus going on the field trip today.") Other students have "recovered" by being given a responsibility or honor that they value, that requires their presence in the classroom. Do not hesitate to ask the school nurse and psychologist for assistance if together you suspect avoidance of academics is the real issue. It is important to keep a child in school on a regular basis, with prompt arrival in the morning, to prevent academic struggles from turning into a case of school refusal. If this does happen, or is at risk of happening, a team approach involving the psychologist, nurse, teacher, and parent will be necessary.

A child's academic embarrassment can hinder self-advocacy

In addition to trying to leave school as discussed above, a child's embarrassment over his academic struggles can lead to other forms of self-defeating behavior. Some of these behaviors can appear positive on the surface. For example, Alejandro tries to cover up by helping his teacher. He'll clean the board, pass out pencils, and take the attendance record to the office. It's great being teacher's right hand man if it means getting away from academic work, and he gets praised for his good citizenship into the bargain. Another behavior that may be positive in the eyes of peers but certainly not in the eyes of the teacher, is to become the class clown, making jokes, pulling stunts, and generally being silly to stop lessons or deflect attention away from his academic performance. If this results in being sent to the principal's office, well it still beats doing fractions. Likewise, not handing in homework (even though she did it but fears the answers may be wrong) makes Shaniqua "independent," not "uncertain" in her mind. If she does not hand in the homework, it cannot earn a poor mark for faulty work (although it may get a zero for not being handed in punctually). Shaniqua may also delude herself that only nerds get good marks; cool kids don't care about grades or handing in homework on time so she must be cool. A teacher may be able to circumvent this issue by grading for effort on homework instead of grading on the accuracy of the answers.

Another form of self-defeating behavior is sitting at the back of the room hoping to go unnoticed. This tends not to work because teachers often walk around the classroom so the back becomes the front in turn. Also, when the child sits at the back, he is more likely to be distracted by the other children or objects in the room. Students who sit up front can see the board better and are primed for interaction with the teacher, thus improving their likelihood of learning. The struggling student generally does not volunteer to answer questions, and rarely raises his or her hand to ask a question or make a comment. When he does not understand something, he just lets it go instead of asking for clarification. This backfires because the student remains confused. Very likely the issue will surface on a test and since the student did not understand the issue he will answer incorrectly. Unbeknownst to a confused student, the odds are that some other children in the room are confused too. It is unlikely that Johnny is the only one who did not "get it." I tell students that if they do not understand something they should ask because they are in school to learn, the point may come up on a test, and they will be helping their classmates too. Struggling students always think they are the "only one" who did not grasp the lesson. I tell them that if they did not understand something, I guarantee there are at least three other children in the room who did not get it either, but they may be even more shy to raise their hands. When Johnny asks, the other students are so relieved that they got another chance. I say, "Johnny, look what a good public service you're doing by asking!"

Students must advocate for their own learning, otherwise they are not taking the leading role in their own education. If a student is too shy to seek clarification of a point in class, he should at least ask the teacher in private later. It is best when a teacher recognizes the student who is afraid to speak up in class and responds supportively. A teacher who does not respond to wrong answers gently, risks making a student even less likely to take a chance on participating in class. It is hard enough to be told your answer is wrong in front of the whole class when you are confident of your academic skills. If you feel incompetent, being publicly told that your answer is wrong can be crushing if it is not said in a kindly, supportive way. There are strategies to encourage students to participate more vigorously in class. These will be considered in Chapter Seven.

Peer relationships in the context of academic difficulties

Struggling students often worry about how their peers think about them. "Everyone laughs at me" is a common complaint. Unfortunately, some teasing and laughing might happen if a student states a wrong answer or makes an irrelevant remark. The teacher needs to discourage such laughter, but most likely cannot prevent all of it. Children are so busy focusing on the time they got laughed at, that they do not notice all the times they took the risk of speaking in class and did not get laughed at.

Often students are too busy worrying what others think to realize that the others are not focusing on them at all.

Sometimes a child hopes to win the affection of a particular peer and is worried that he won't look good to him or her. "Betsy won't like me because I'm in the slow math group." If that is true, then Betsy is shallow and not worthy of your child's friendship. More likely, Betsy likes your son just fine. If she doesn't, it is because he always beats her in checkers, or perhaps accidentally pushed her on the playground and she mistakenly believed it was done on purpose. She never even thought about his math group.

"None of the smart kids play with me. My friends are dummies, too. Only the dummies play with me." Such comments suggest the child believes he has no social status, no respect from his peers. Observation around the classroom and at recess often reveals this to be untrue. Many high achieving students play happily with the less academically successful because they pick their friends according to their personality, kindness, and common interests, not their grades. The struggling student may be so focused on his reading weakness that he forgets he is admired for his prowess with a soccer ball, his skill on the piano, or the artistic quality of his drawing. He forgets that others like him just for who he is. It is also important for a school's administration to showcase students' non-academic talents in music, art, sports, citizenship, etc., and not only to reward students for academic performance. This supports students emotionally, and boosts their confidence and willingness to address the areas they find more challenging.

Fears of punishment

Sometimes children fear that their parents will punish them for poor marks. They fear missing their friends' birthday parties, losing their allowance, or getting a spanking. Such punishment is not going to work. You cannot make someone achieve academically by punishing him. If you could, all students would be stellar. Students who are not spending an appropriate amount of time studying due to too many hours playing video games, watching TV, etc., may need more guidance, structure, or rules regarding play time and study time. This is not a punishment (although some children may need help understanding it) because the video games and TV are still allowed, just with moderation. For example, TV shows can be recorded and watched on weekends or after homework is completed. It will be easier, more productive, and make for a more cooperative, peaceful household if the siblings follow the "homework first, TV in moderation" rule too, even if they are performing satisfactorily.

Fear can lead to giving up

Some struggling students become so frustrated that they give up and back away from scholastic tasks. They think, "if I don't try, I can't fail." It is vital to keep motivation alive. Recognition of effort, not just of success, is the key to fostering hope, a positive attitude, and a willingness to persist.

Sometimes, students set unrealistically high goals for themselves, guaranteeing failure. These students need to be guided toward realistic challenges so that they may both grow and experience success. It's all very well to tell students to "reach for the stars," but a fair number of those stars need in fact to be within reach.

Fear for the future

Some children are so very anxious about their academic weaknesses that they exaggerate the situation. They worry that the situation will never change, that they will always struggle in school. They fear that they will not get into college or get a good job. They fear that they are letting their parents down, that "they love my brother more because he gets straight A's." These children not only need to learn effective study skills and to see academic progress, they also need psychological counseling to support a positive self-regard and develop the strength to tackle their challenges. Their parents should attend counseling as well since their participation and cooperation are vital. It would be best to keep the teacher in the loop as well.

Psychological counseling

Psychological counseling is a safe place where a child may share his deepest fears and learn to face, address, and deflate them with the psychologist's help. In counseling, the psychologist works to help the student see when his fears are erroneous, exaggerated, and hinder his academic progress. The psychologist can teach the student relaxation techniques that can be employed in class, while taking a test or during homework time whenever the student starts to feel anxious. Together, psychologist and student can explore various study skills and focus on the ones most compatible with the student's needs and personality. The psychologist can help the student recognize academic progress, even small steps, and take pride in them and his achievements. The child can learn to see himself as a competent student instead of an incompetent one.

Key points from Chapter Two:

1. Your child may have ineffective study skills even though he tries hard.
2. Children have strong feelings about academics and themselves.
3. You need to be alert for school avoidance behaviors.
4. Embarrassment hinders children from acting in self-advocating ways.
5. Children worry what peers think of their academic performance.
6. Children worry that their parents will punish them for poor academic performance.

7. Children worry that their academic difficulties will affect their future regarding school, work, and family relationships.

Questions for parents to pursue:

1. Have you discussed your child's feelings about academics with him?
2. In what way does your son study ineffectively?
3. What study skills does your daughter lack?
4. How does your child feel about going to school?
5. Does your child think his teacher is supportive?
6. Do other children tease or laugh at your child's mistakes?
7. Is your child advocating for himself or standing in his own way?
8. How much time does your child spend studying?

CHAPTER THREE

PARENTS HAVE STRONG FEELINGS THAT CAN INTERFERE WITH THEIR CHILD'S PROGRESS

Denial of the problem

No parent wants his or her child to have academic difficulties. School problems can be so upsetting and consume so much parental time that the urge to avoid them can be strong. At some point in life, haven't we all wished that some problem would "just go away?" It is completely natural for you to wish that your child's learning problem would just go away. Believe me, your child wishes it even harder than you do. Unfortunately, just wishing won't make it so.

Jay's father told his teacher, "Jay doesn't have a problem. I was a late bloomer and I turned out okay. My two other kids were late bloomers and caught up. Jay will be fine later." Sometimes this is true—there are late bloomers—but often it is not true. How long can you afford to wait to find out? The foundation blocks of learning must be solidly in place for subsequent learning to be accomplished. Adding new academic material when the old material is not securely mastered results in a confused student who is limited in what he or she can grasp and pursue. It is easier to address a small problem than a big, entrenched one.

"Maybe we should change schools." You can't run away from the academic problems. They will re-surface at the new school sooner or later if they have not been addressed appropriately. Changing schools will not magically enable your child to multiply three-digit numbers. While there are times when a fresh start may be advisable, parents need to know whether the proposed new school has the academic support programs suitable for their child. A transfer without appropriate support is more likely to repeat history than to ameliorate matters.

Parents might consider a fresh start when sincere efforts to work with the original school have not been successful or if the student is suffering socially from his learning difficulties. Sometimes another school is a better match for a particular student.

Nonetheless, for many parents, transferring to another school is not an option. There may not be another school that meets zoning legalities, is geographically practical, affordable, philosophically acceptable to the family, or that will accept the student.

"I don't have time for this. I'm busy. I have to work long hours. Junior has to solve his own problems." Junior would like to solve his academic problems more than anything but he cannot do it alone. Research indicates that the brain is more pliable at a younger age. Waiting for help closes the window of opportunity and makes learning harder later. Junior needs your help very much right now. You are a vital component of the solution and Junior dearly wants your help.

Parents may feel their social status is low

It is hard not to be envious when you hear other parents discussing the picnic for the gifted class when your child is not doing well in school. You feel low on the totem pole when your nephew's report card shows A's, your niece's fluency gets her elected president of the French club, but your daughter does not have a special achievement for you to brag about. Instead of excitedly sharing your Lulu's science award, you worry that she will be held back and not promoted with her classmates. Are you worried about Lulu's possible retention because of her feelings or because of how you will feel when you have to tell the other mothers in your circle? Do you worry that they will look down on you if Lulu is not promoted? Do you fear they will laugh behind your back if Lulu has to attend summer school? Will they think you are a "bad mother?" All of these feelings and thoughts are understandable and shared by many parents. Nonetheless, do not let such feelings and thoughts interfere with making decisions that, after careful consideration, you know are in your child's best interests.

Blaming the child

A frustrated father said to me "My wife and I never had school problems," thus implying that the fault lies strictly with the child. You are fortunate that you had a smooth school experience, but your child is not you. He is his own person and he may have strengths in other areas that you lack.

"Junior only works if he likes a subject; he's not motivated." It is hard to persevere when you feel discouraged, when you don't see your efforts rewarded. It is especially hard to persevere in a subject that you do not like, probably because it is extra hard for you. This may be a chicken-egg situation as it is hard to know which came first, the difficulty or the dislike. Unfortunately, they reinforce each other to the child's disadvantage.

"She should just do her job as a student and get on with it." She would if she could. Lulu lacks study skills, is missing foundation pieces, and doesn't understand how to help herself. She's not "making trouble" for the fun of it. She needs support and guidance.

"My son's just lazy, that's why he's doing poorly. Just lazy." Your boy is not likely to be any lazier than anyone else. Children (and adults) are full of energy and focus for what they want to do and for what they can do. Look at Roberta and Ginger running fast to catch a ball and score a point, look at Alan and James enthusiastically banging a drum in response to the music teacher's baton. Neil spends hours patiently building model airplanes. Some people are better at harnessing their energy and directing it where it needs to go than others are, but with the right supports and guidance, the skill can be learned.

Blaming the teacher

"My child would do fine in school if he had a better teacher." Parents have expressed to me a variety of feelings along this line. The teacher is too young, the teacher is too old. He is too strict, he is not strict enough. She is too inexperienced, she has been teaching for too long and should retire. The class has too many students in it and the teacher gives too much attention to the other kids. Junior doesn't like Mrs. Smith; she's mean. "Mrs. Smith doesn't like my Junior and I don't like Mrs. Smith either." Mrs. Smith can't teach; her lessons are boring. Her lessons are too hard, too simple, too complicated, too long, too short. "I'm a parent but I used to be a teacher so I know." One group of parents adores Mrs. Smith while the other group excoriates her. There will be a classroom full of parents and no consensus.

The teacher is the one who told you that Junior is having a rough time at his lessons. The teacher is the one who burst your bubble. It's awfully tempting to shoot the messenger, but doing so won't make Junior read any more fluently. If you disparage the teacher, your child will lose respect for her, which will hinder his ability to respond to instruction. Blaming the teacher is unhelpful and does not promote an understanding of the full picture. It is in your child's best interest for you to work with the teacher as a constructive team. If the teacher should need any guidance about teaching your child, it is preferable and appropriate for his or her supervisor to address the issue.

Sometimes parents blame each other

Comments from parents have also reflected a tendency to blame the spouse, lest the blamer be the "guilty" party. "Learning problems run in my husband's side of the family." "My wife is too strict with our child," or the converse "my husband is too lenient with our child." "My husband travels on business so much that he won't be the bad guy when he's home; I always have to say no TV until you've done your homework." It sounds to me that you feel the responsibility for dealing with your child's issue all falls on just you. Nonetheless, spouses should not blame each other. Blaming doesn't solve the issue; it just makes parents feel worse. You need to be unified to successfully support your child. Do discuss your expectations regarding your child and his school work with your spouse and be clear about what you want and do not want (e.g., Junior will spend a minimum of one hour on his homework before he is allowed to watch TV; if friends call, Junior is not allowed to speak on the telephone during the homework hour).

Clear expectations are also important when other adults are involved. "The babysitter doesn't make Junior do his homework" is not an explanation. You cannot abdicate responsibility and blame the babysitter. She works for you. The babysitter needs you to clarify your expectations of her, advise her on how to achieve them, and support her authority with your children.

It is more complicated when there are siblings in addition to the struggling learner. If any of those siblings also have learning issues, the complication increases further. In any case, it is true as parents say, that they need to give time to the other children as well. The challenged learner cannot have all the attention, especially as it may lead to the siblings feeling that their achievements are ignored or unrewarded. It is hard to be a parent and feel pulled in several directions at once. While you are reading to the baby, it gives your second grader a chance to practice his spelling words, so he can demonstrate his progress after you finish the baby's picture book. Encourage the children to be appreciative audience members when each takes a turn at sharing what he or she learned with the family.

Blaming yourself

While some parents blame the child, each other, or the school, other parents blame themselves. "I must be doing something wrong." No. The only thing that would be wrong would be to ignore the problem and not take constructive steps to help your child. "I don't make enough money, I don't have a college degree." There are plenty of children who struggle academically even though their parents are more educated or wealthy than you are. There is no automatic protection. "I'm a bad mother." No, you are not. Just as you are not a bad mother if your child has allergies, you are not a bad mother if your child needs extra help in school. You are a worried mother, a concerned mother, a loving mother, a mother eager to help.

You are going to do all you can to help your child perform satisfactorily in school, so you are a good mother.

"It's my fault my kid has trouble because my English is limited. We don't speak English at home. We immigrated here." Immigration did not necessarily cause your child's difficulty. It is possible that had you remained in your home country, your child would still have experienced learning problems there. Having to learn English complicates the picture for your child but he can learn English. You can still support, encourage, and advocate for your child even if your English is limited. Ask the teacher, psychologist or principal if there are staff members or other parents who speak your native language and to put you in touch with them. They may be able to help you understand and negotiate school procedures, and make you feel more comfortable. Additionally, if you enroll in an English course, you will set a fine first-hand example for your child about the importance of learning.

"I want to help my daughter but I can't explain the homework. I don't get fractions either." This can be embarrassing but does not need to prevent you from helping your child. You can coach and encourage even if you don't know the content area, just as you can listen to and encourage violin practice even if you don't know how to play. Together you and your daughter can look at examples in the textbook to use as models for solving the homework problems. There are also homework help hotlines and websites. Ask the school librarian for appropriate websites for your child's grade level. You can guide your daughter through a practical procedure of how to figure out problems and answer questions even if you are not familiar with a specific subject. There may also be someone else at home who is better able to assist with math. Your forte may be history.

"I don't know what to do to help my child." You've already started to help your child by reading this book. You are thinking about her academic struggles and starting to research steps you can take to help her overcome them.

You may feel disappointed

Parents dream about how their children will turn out. They picture them strong, tall, athletic, musical, artistic, and scholastically excellent. Acknowledging that the child has a weak area is to acknowledge disappointment that your fantasy is not reality. It is not always easy to accept that your dream did not come true. It is hard, but necessary, to let go of the fantasy child and enjoy the real one, with his weaknesses and strengths combined. It is necessary for you to be realistic about the area in which your child requires support. This permits him to receive it and maximize his potential.

Perhaps you had hoped your child would excel at foreign languages because you did not. You cannot live vicariously through your child. Your achievements are yours and his are his. It is all right for your child to have different strengths and weaknesses from yours. It could turn out that your child has some strengths that will serve him more significantly later in life than will academic excellence. Some experts believe that social skills and work ethic are more important in the long run than high marks in school.

It is very hard to hear that one's child has a weakness and there is a tendency to deny it. This is because it often feels like a criticism of oneself. There is also a natural inclination to blame others for the problem. Eventually, it is best to accept that your child is his or her own person with unique strengths and weaknesses. We all have weaknesses as it is part of being human. Don't waste time feeling guilty for nothing. Use your energy to obtain appropriate academic support for your student.

Key points from Chapter Three:

1. Sometimes parents try to deny that their child has a problem with academics.
2. Parents may feel embarrassed socially when others speak about their children's academic achievements.
3. Sometimes parents blame the child for having difficulty.
4. Sometimes parents blame each other for the child's academic difficulty.
5. There are parents who blame themselves.
6. It is normal to have strong feelings about your child and his situation.
7. You may feel disappointed that your child does not match your fantasy of how he would be. Accepting your child for who he is allows you both to move forward.

Questions for parents to pursue:

1. Can you acknowledge your child's problem?
2. Are you embarrassed in front of your friends?
3. Do you blame your child (e.g., "lazy kid")?
4. Are you blaming your spouse?
5. Have you been blaming yourself for your child's struggles?
6. Can you accept that the perfect fantasy child is just that, a fantasy?
7. Are you able to see your child as he or she is, weaknesses and strengths?

CHAPTER FOUR

YOUR SCHOOL EXPERIENCE MAY NOT MATCH YOUR CHILD'S

Grandparents' views may have differed from yours

It is possible that your parents' views or your spouse's parents' views about school were different from the views you have now in reference to your own children. The grandparents may not have worried about school achievement so much due to life experiences involving immediate survival, such as poverty, immigration, serious illness or war. They may have stressed the importance of earning rather than learning. This could have been due to cultural values, personal preferences or economic necessity.

Concerns regarding employment may have been different than they are now. Perhaps the grandparents worked in a family business that guaranteed employment. It is possible that academic excellence or higher education was not relevant to the ability to run the business or not required, because your generation had assured employment upon coming of age. The grandparents may have been more concerned about problems found outside the classroom.

In some families, a university education was not expected or particularly valued. In some quarters, it may have been seen as impractical, whereas vocational training was seen as useful. Society needs skilled auto mechanics, hairdressers, tailors, plumbers, electricians, welders, etc. These occupations do not require a college degree but are highly in demand. They require a different type of educational training and are obvious in their employment opportunities throughout life.

The grandparent generation may also have differed in their educational expectations for boys versus girls or older children versus younger ones. An older child may have been sent to college because he was the first born, and therefore given higher status than the other siblings. Conversely, the older children may not have been able to attend because the grandparents couldn't afford it. The older children may have had to work to contribute income for the family. By the time the grandparents could afford tuition, it was too late for the older children, so the younger ones went to college. It is also possible that the grandparents may have rationed expensive education, aware that some of their offspring were more likely to benefit from it than others, due to different levels of intelligence, motivation, talent, or interest. Girls may not have been able to attend because it was assumed they would marry and have babies and not work outside the home, thus "wasting" a college degree. With the above mindset, the grandparents may have not worried so much about a child who was not an academic success as long as he could contribute to the family in other useful ways.

In contrast, for some families, the parents' views about academics and the grandparents' views may be completely in agreement. Here, the

pressure may be to produce yet another generation of fine scholars in keeping with family tradi-
tion. Just as you don't want your son to be the
generation that broke the treasured heirloom vase
handed down from his great-great-grandmother,
you don't want him to be the non-scholar in a
family that reveres learning and academic achievement. You may still feel this way even if your son
displays an admired talent not generally found
among your relatives. The pressure to keep up can
be as intense as the pressure to be the pioneer.

With each generation, the times, views, and
circumstances can change. What was important
while you were growing up may be less so now
and what was less stressed during your childhood
may be much more important now when you are
an adult. Consider how the use of computers,
cell phones, iPods, and other similar gadgets has
spread throughout society. There are computer-
related careers now that were non-existent not all
that long ago. You cannot change the circumstances under which you grew up, just realize that they
may be different from what your child experiences
now. You can only focus on what you believe is in
your child's best interests given the world in which
we live today and what you value for tomorrow.

You may have completed school easily

It is hard to truly understand how something can be
difficult for someone else when we find it so simple.
Those of us who completed school without difficulty and saw many other children likewise sailing

smoothly along, may find it hard to fully grasp the feelings of a child who struggles in the classroom.

Perhaps you recall occasional academic struggles in an otherwise calm school experience. Maybe French verbs made you scream or perhaps you tore your hair out over dividing mixed numerals. Maybe you even got a poor mark or failed a test somewhere along the line. As upsetting and frustrating as an occasional failure can be, it is completely different from feeling that school life is an uphill battle each and every day. A student who is normally successful but has the odd failure believes he can study some more and overcome the problem. The student who is often stymied is at risk of losing hope as he has not been successful frequently enough to believe in his efforts.

It is said that one must walk a mile in another person's shoes in order to understand him. I participated in some enlightening workshops intended to simulate what it is like to have various disabilities. For example, one task was to read from a book while looking through a piece of paper that had a few small unevenly spaced holes in it. This was intended to simulate a visual impairment. Another exercise was to stuff cotton or earplugs in your ears and try to listen to and understand a lecture, simulating an auditory deficit. Other exercises involved placing semi-opaque paper over your glasses, trying to write quickly with the non-dominant hand, and attempting to run a race with a weight strapped to one leg. One exercise, an attempt to simulate trying to learn with Attention Deficit Hyperactivity Disorder, involved trying to listen to and remember information that the "teacher" was saying, while being distracted by lively visual and auditory effects in the room or out the window. It would be difficult to create simulation exercises for every type of learning issue, but you understand the idea. You might want to pause here and try out a few of the above exercises on yourself. I am sure you will gain a new perspective on tasks you perform routinely.

You may have had academic difficulties

While some parents studied and went through their school days easily, others did not. You may recall your own struggles in the classroom and fear for your child. If you struggled in school, you may be blaming yourself as the cause of your child's difficulties. As discussed above, this is not a matter of fault, and blaming yourself is not going to help. Use your energy, combined with your personal experience of what helped you and what did not, to obtain academic support for your child.

Parents who had a rough time learning have many upsetting memories from their school days. If this is you, you may remember feeling ashamed when you could not answer a question or were laughed at by other children. Perhaps you suffered the humiliation of having to repeat a grade while your friends were promoted. You had to study in the same class with your best friend's younger sister, or worse with your own. You lost status not only in school, but also at home, a deep source of embarrassment.

Perhaps you feel that you never properly resolved

your academic difficulties. You graduated, worked, married, and had your own kids, but certain circumstances still cause you some anxiety. When you go out for coffee and cake with your friends, do you fear having to calculate the tip? Do you worry that you will accidentally offend the waiter? Do you just say to the group "tell me what I owe" and trust them to get it right? When shopping for new clothes, do you have trouble figuring out the final price when the sign says "20% discount?" In the supermarket, are you unsure which cereal is more expensive? Do you stumble and get nervous when you have to read instructions or fill out forms? Do you fear that your daughter or son will suffer this pressure throughout her or his life too?

Your school may not have offered the supports your child's school does

Given your own experience, it is understandable that faced with your child's academic struggle, you think that since nothing really helped you, likewise nothing will help Junior. This is a fair concern but times have changed.

Social attitudes that impact teaching have changed. There was a time when a struggling student was dismissed as "dull," "lazy," or "bad." Now, educators are aware that different children learn in different ways. There are advances in how to teach. Some children learn better when the lesson is presented visually, while others respond better to auditory instruction. Still others require kinesthetic input to grasp concepts. Differentiated instruction is common, with more one-to-one attention. Class sizes are smaller in many schools now, compared to what they were in past generations. Some people told me that their childhood classes contained forty students and one teacher. Today, twenty-five students, a teacher and often a teaching assistant is the more likely situation.

Laws pertaining to education have changed too. In 1975, Public Law 94-142 granted all children a "free and appropriate" public school education in the United States. There have been advances in laws regarding the education of special education students as well as students at risk (Response to Intervention was included in the 2004 re-authorization of the Individuals with Disabilities Education Act). Now you are the parent of a school-age child, but when you were growing up, public school support services were still in development. If you attended private school, the school may not have been required to provide any extra help. Support services and awareness of their importance have evolved considerably over the years.

The school your child attends may be very different from the one you went to. Perhaps you attended public school and your son goes to a private school. Perhaps you attended a private school but send your daughter to a public school. Your child's school may have different resources, different expectations, and a different emphasis than your school had. Your school may have stressed religious studies while your child's school may focus more on standard academic subjects. Your child's school may be more concerned with preparing students for eventual university studies or place greater emphasis on art or music than your school did. Even if it's the same school, times have changed and the school's administration may have a different philosophy or a different direction, and may offer more support services for students who need them than it did in the past.

It is not just schools that have changed over the course of a generation. Communities also change, along with the resources available. Public libraries are often a source of educational support material, whether it consists of books, websites, or tutoring offered by neighborhood volunteers. There may be relevant academic support services available through local organizations such as the "Y," "Boys and Girls Club," a "teen center," a church, or private institutions of study such as Huntington Learning Center. These are just some examples and are neither endorsements nor criticisms of these institutions. Neighborhoods differ as to the variety and quality of available community resources.

When you think about school, classes, and homework, you tend to think of your own experience first. Your childhood experience naturally forms the baseline for comparisons with your child's school life. It is important to remember that your own parents may have had different pressures and priorities than you are currently facing as a parent. This may have given them a different perspective regarding education than yours. Your child's school may differ from the one you attended in terms of class size, teacher training, philosophy, attitudes, and available resources. Nowadays, society is generally more understanding of the student who needs extra support.

Key points from Chapter Four:

1. The student's grandparents may have held different views about academics than his parents currently hold.
2. The grandparents' life circumstances may have been different from those in which the child is currently being raised.
3. The parents may not have had any academic difficulties. This can make it hard to appreciate what a struggling student goes through.
4. There are simulation exercises to help one gain the perspective of a struggling student.
5. A parent might have struggled herself, leading to fear for the child's future.
6. The child's school may be quite different from the parent's school.
7. Community supports, social attitudes, and public law have changed.

Questions for parents to pursue:

1. What do you know or remember of your parents' views about education?
2. Did your parents support your pursuit of education?
3. What was your school experience? Did you progress smoothly or struggle academically?
4. How do you relate to your child's experience?
5. Compare your school with your child's school.
6. What resources are available to your child in the community?

CHAPTER FIVE

PARENTS MUST TAKE THE LEAD AT HOME

Provide a structured home

In order for your child to function academically at a successful level, he needs the support of a structured home. The structure reinforces that the family values school work as a top priority.

A structured home is clean and tidy to a reasonable degree and family members can find the items they need for school work or other activities. The student has a quiet, practical place to do his or her homework. There is a desk or table, a firm but comfortable desk chair, and drawers, files, boxes, shelves, or other containers to store necessary school materials. The necessary school materials include such items as paper, pencils, pens, ruler, calculator, dictionary, textbooks, workbooks, and more often than not, a computer.

Set up a schedule for homework, activities such as music lessons or sports, and chores. Do not schedule more activities than the child can handle. There needs to be ample study time and a reasonable amount of "down time" in which to rest. If Junior's marks are not satisfactory or if he is often tired or cranky, it can be a sign that he is overextended.

Jane is a ten-year-old fifth grader. Jane's schedule is typed and illustrated, posted on her bedroom door, and reads as follows:

Jane's After School Schedule:

3:30- school bus arrives at home.
3:30 to 4:00 -eat snack, play with dog, relax with family.
4:00 to 5:00- do homework.
5:00 to 5:30- practice the piano.
5:30 to 6:00-do chores (e.g., set the table, tear lettuce for salad, and clean up her room).
6:00 to 7:00- dinner time with family.
7:00-7:30- study time or reading time.
7:30- 8:00 - free time.
8:00- bath time and bed time.

If Jane has a test coming up, she will study from 7:00 to 7:30; if there is no test, she will work on a long-term homework project or read. During her free time from 7:30 to 8:00, Jane might watch a TV show or play checkers with her brother. Eight o'clock means bath time followed by bedtime. Different school schedules and family requirements, along with the age of the child, will guide the creation of a specific student's schedule.

Jane's brother, Dick, is only six and has very little homework from his first grade class. Nonetheless, he knows the rule: Do not disturb Jane during homework and study times. Dick will do his homework when Jane does hers. Since he finishes sooner, his duties are then to read a book, play outside, draw a picture, or do some activity with mother that will be part of "quiet time in the house."

Likewise, Jane knows that should she finish her work early, she is not to disturb Dick when he is working.   If mother knows that the schedule will be disrupted—such as for the children's dental appointments—she will work with the children in advance to create a revised schedule for the day, giving priority to schoolwork. Weekend time may be needed for any long-term homework assignment or to catch up on music practice and chores.

Parents can find practical and creative ways to support their child's study schedule.   Use technology to your family's advantage. TV shows can be recorded and watched after homework is done or on weekends.   Likewise, a telephone or computer chat time can be built into the schedule to preserve the benefits of socializing without interrupting study time.   Parents need to help their child develop a schedule that will support the child and also serve the family's particular needs in a practical way.

Consider physical and medical impact

In addition to providing a clean and organized home, parents also support their child by cooking and serving healthy, nutritious foods to enable physical and mental growth.   While a reasonable number of fast food meals and sugary snacks will not cause harm, the major portion of the child's diet should be wholesome and healthy for proper brain function.   Involving your child in choosing some of the menu can facilitate cooperation from a picky eater.   Having your child help you grow vegetables in your yard or in a pot can become an educational as well as a culinary experience.

Appropriate care also includes regular medical and dental check-ups. When there are difficulties in learning, it is vital to rule out any deficiencies in vision or hearing. Kate kept stumbling over words when she read from the blackboard. She stopped volunteering to read and appeared to withdraw from the lesson. It turned out she could not see the board clearly. A pair of glasses restored her enthusiasm for class and enabled her to progress. Although less common, some children require hearing aids. The need to hear sounds and words accurately in order to develop language skills, gather information, and process classroom discussion cannot be overstated. If a child has a history of frequent ear infections or colds, it would be in his best interests to discuss not just a hearing test but a full audiological evaluation with his physician.

Some children have medical conditions that require various medications. Sometimes, a student experiences a side effect from the medicine that hinders his or her ability to learn. For example, some asthma medications can make children restless. If you have a concern about your child's medicine, discuss it with your physician. Do not stop prescribed medication on your own as this could impair your child's health. A different medicine may be more suited to your child's needs.

There are also cases where a child is diagnosed with a condition that interferes with learning and that is typically treated with medication, but the parents are reluctant to put their child on medication. This situation often arises in the case of an Attention Deficit Disorder or other neurological or psychiatric disorders. I am neither advocating for medication nor advocating against it. Public school staff members are often prohibited from requiring that parents medicate their child although private school staff may be able to make greater demands. I have seen many cases where medication did wonders for the student's ability to focus and rein in distracting behaviors. Jordan turned himself around in second grade after starting medication. His teachers' comments on his report cards read like night and day. I have also seen cases where students did not respond effectively and several different medications had to be tried before an appropriate one was found (or in some cases before the parents decided to forego it). Every school year there are parents who tell me that they do not want to medicate their child "because there are consequences to giving medication." Yes, there are consequences to giving medication. There are also consequences of *not* giving medication. Both giving and not giving medication can have positive and negative consequences. Nonetheless, I rarely hear parents hesitate to provide medication for a non-psychiatric disorder, such as diabetes, asthma, or sore throat. While I understand parents' concerns, it is not fair to the student to refuse to consider an option that may be just what the child needs. I do recommend that parents keep an open mind, and have a frank discussion with a physician who specializes in children with such disorders. Whether or not a particular child should take medication is a decision that should be made between his parents and their physician.

There are other therapeutic treatments apart from medication that may be beneficial to your child. DaShawn, a first grade student, struggled with fine motor skills such as holding a pencil and cutting with scissors. His parents took him to an Occupational Therapist to develop his grasping and visual-motor integration skills. Karen, a second grade student, attended speech therapy in order to build vocabulary and improve her understanding of how grammar indicates meaning. Xavier, a third grader, was having notable difficulty with reading. His mother took him to a Vision Therapist who worked with Xavier to teach him how to control his eye movements so that he could track and focus better. Many children of my acquaintance have improved their functioning as a result of various therapies. Nonetheless, please note that not every form of therapy offered is necessarily reputable or appropriate for your child. I advise consulting with your School Psychologist and pediatrician before arranging private therapy for your child.

In the cases described above, it was the parents who arranged and paid for their children to attend private therapies to support their educational progress. Paying for private therapies often incurs some cost, even with insurance. I know parents who cut back on expenses or worked an extra job to pay the fees. Sometimes, even one or two sessions with a therapist can be helpful to give advice and strategies to practice at home, if weekly sessions are too expensive. Another alternative is a local college with a clinic where interns offer free therapy as they train. Some therapists offer sliding fees depending on the parents' income. If parents opt to work with a private therapist, they may need to do some research to find the way that works best for their family.

Go the extra mile

In addition to paying for medical or therapeutic treatments, parents have other ways of contributing to their child's educational progress. Ask your child about his homework every day. Although you should not do it for him, discussing a confusing point or explaining something is appropriate. If your child cannot complete the work without considerable help, send a note to the teacher as such a situation suggests that the unit may need to be re-taught. It is possible that other students in the class also have difficulty with the homework.

If Junior misses school due to illness, help him to catch up what he missed. There are several ways to do this. Junior can call a friend to find out the assignments he missed. He can check online if the teacher posts assignments on the school website. Junior can meet with his teacher before school or after school to review missed lessons. It is important that the returning student learn missed material promptly or he will be at a disadvantage as the lessons proceed. Meeting with the teacher outside of class time demonstrates the child's motivation to learn and encourages the teacher to view him positively.

Similarly, do not pull a struggling learner out of school unnecessarily. Schedule routine dentist appointments after school and take family vacations when school is closed. Likewise, do not let your child stay up late on a school night. If you are invited to a special event, either leave early or have your child stay home with a babysitter who will put her to bed at the appropriate time. A tired student cannot learn properly. Sleeping in and then arriving two hours late to school still means two hours of valuable class time were missed.

There are times when the parent must inconvenience himself. When she was a middle school student, my older daughter hit a rough spot in math. I drove her to school at 6:50 am every day so she could meet with her teacher for extra help. Did either of us want to get up at 6:00 am? No, but the effort paid off. Sandra sailed forward in math. Her teacher duly noted her steady efforts to help herself learn, and I was very proud of her progress. Although getting up extra early was an inconvenience, I reframed it in my mind as an "investment" in my daughter, an investment that paid a large dividend for her.

If your child is struggling in class, it is best to stay in touch with his or her teacher on a frequent, regular basis. This can be accomplished by email or via a communication notebook which the parent and teacher send back and forth. Do not wait for the report card to see how Junior is doing as he could lose a lot of ground by then (neither should the teacher use the report card as the first indication of a problem). If you have a concern, schedule an appointment with the teacher to learn how Junior is functioning in class, and how you and the teacher can work together to support his learning. This avoids surprises and can prevent little problems from growing into big ones. You may need to take time off from work, or make arrangements to come to school very early in the morning, but making the effort is important for your child.

You can also support your child by being involved in school activities, learning more about the curriculum, and finding out what your child will be studying in the following year. Attend Parent Teacher Association (PTA) meetings, science fairs, and music concerts, even if your child's work is not included, to obtain an overall picture of what is expected at school. If you can, volunteer in the classroom, even if only occasionally, to read to the students, teach them about a skill you have, or help the teacher as needed. Young students are eager for the attention of adults and enjoy showing off their skills in reading or art projects. One school where I worked held an annual Reading Day, when non-classroom staff members were invited to read stories to elementary classes. I had a blast; the students were so eager. It was the best day of the school year.

Another way to show support for your child is to become a student too. Is there something that you would like to learn? Mrs. Martinez enrolled in English class and sat down to her homework alongside her daughter when she did her school work. Seeing her mother study inspired little Maria. Mother and daughter encouraged each other when either got confused.

Keep your frustration away from your child

There will be times when you will feel quite frustrated or angry regarding your son's academic struggles. Such feelings are natural but you want to keep them away from your child because hearing them will make him more upset and hinder his progress. Vent your feelings and thoughts to your spouse, your best friend, your sister, a therapist or a member of the clergy. Be sure to speak where you will not be overheard. Writing in a diary is also an appropriate way to express frustration, just keep the diary away from where your child or others might find it.

If you have concerns regarding how Junior's teacher is working with him, speak with the teacher for details. If your concerns persist, you could request a meeting with the principal. Do not criticize the teacher or undermine her in the process as you and your child may have to continue working with her. You do not want the school staff to see you as a difficult, obstructionist parent, as they will be less inclined to work with you. It can be hard to know if the teacher is not teaching in a way that meets Junior's needs, if Junior is not doing the best that he could do, if there is a personality conflict, or all of the above. Changing Junior's class is a big step. While I have seen this work out well at times, it carries some significant risks. One risk is that it sends your child the message that his learning difficulty is the teacher's fault, that he has no responsibility to make an effort. A second risk is the message that says you can run away from your problems. Junior may find he does not perform any better with the new teacher. The third risk to your child is the message that others will bail him out, that he does not need to find solutions to help himself. As there may not be another class to switch Junior into, the ability to work with what one has, even under less than ideal circumstances, is a valuable life lesson.

Continue to seek constructive advice to help your child learn. You have already started to do so by reading this book. Stay on the look out for other books, articles, professionals, websites or television programs that address the issue. You can never learn too much about supporting your child educationally.

Be encouraging

Junior's learning difficulty took time to develop and will take time to overcome. It is important to be realistic about the pace of progress and to appreciate the small victories along the way. Praise your child, acknowledge his efforts, express your pleasure at the little steps, not just the big ones. Sam now remembers to start sentences with capital letters—great! Jill used to get only two out of ten spelling words right and on last Friday's quiz she got six—wonderful! Post those papers on the refrigerator for all the family to see. Make a copy and send it to Grandmother. Share the progress and the joy. Your child will beam.

Let your child "accidentally" overhear you brag about him and his progress. Just "happen" to tell Aunt Betty that Roger correctly added five problems with two-digit numbers when he's playing nearby. When you're on the phone to your cousin Joan, mention Lulu's progress in reading just as she comes into the kitchen for a glass of water. Brag as if you didn't know Lulu was there. Watch her try to drink water and grin at the same time!

Never let a sibling, other relative or anyone else tease your child about his or her learning challenges or low marks. If siblings do this, it creates a poisonous atmosphere in the house and damages the child's willingness to work. Don't compare your child's school performance to that of his or her siblings or allow others to either. (I know we all compare in our thoughts but don't say comparisons aloud.) Barbara is all too well aware that her older sister is brilliant and that the teachers her sister once had now expect so much from her. Encourage siblings and others to see your child's strengths, one of which is working to address his weaknesses. Aaron may be confused about subtraction with regrouping but he may be a whiz at baseball or a very good clarinet player.

Insist that relevant people adhere to the plan

It is imperative that other people involved in your child's care, such as your spouse, aunt, grandparents and babysitter, all be on the same page regarding his academic support. The babysitter must enforce the no teasing rule. She must be sure the children do their homework before they watch television or play on their computers. If

Grandpa agreed to drive Junior to his after school tutoring, he must not start grumbling about it in front of Junior. Have Aunt Amy post Junior's creative writing exercise on her refrigerator so he can delight in seeing it when he visits her. With your lead, others will follow to support the student.

Parents play a vital role in supporting their child educationally. They do this by taking the lead at home and providing an encouraging, support-ive, helpful environment. Going the extra mile to obtain any needed therapeutic treatment or pitch-ing in at school pays back efforts in your student's progress.

Key points from Chapter Five:

1. Provide a structured home.
2. Provide appropriate medical or therapeutic care.
3. Go the extra mile. Be involved with your child's school.
4. Make sure your son or daughter catches up missed work.
5. Take your child in early for tutoring when needed.
6. Keep your frustration away from your child.
7. Be encouraging, even of small steps.
8. Insist that others adhere to your plan to support your child.

Questions for parents to pursue:

1. Does your child have an orderly, quiet place to study?
2. Does your child have the necessary materials close at hand?
3. Are medical and dental appointments up to date?
4. Does your child eat a nutritious diet?
5. If relevant, is your child getting any needed therapeutic support?
6. Are you involved in your child's school?
7. Do you go the extra mile even if you are inconvenienced?
8. Are you keeping your frustrations away from your child?
9. Are you encouraging and praising your child?
10. Do you insist other relevant people adhere to your plan to support your child?

CHAPTER SIX

TIME AND RESOURCE MANAGEMENT

Preparing for homework

Many children think that "doing their homework" involves a lot of time and suffering. Depending on the school, teacher, or grade, it might involve a lot of time, but need not involve suffering. Effort, yes; suffering, no. Homework is supposed to be an opportunity for students to practice and reinforce information or skills taught in class. It is not supposed to be the student's first exposure to the material. If a student is suffering in doing his or her homework, it may be because of incorrect or inefficient study skills. Fortunately, students can learn to study effectively.

Study skills begin with self-advocacy. Junior needs to arrive to class on time, with his books, and pay attention. He should actively participate in the lesson. This means listening carefully, following the discussion, and making connections to previously learned material or personal experiences. It also means extrapolating how the information could be applied in different circumstances. Junior needs to think ahead and make predictions, and note how the material unfolds compared to his predictions. Actively making relevant comments keeps a student engaged and demonstrates his interest and intention to learn. Junior needs to raise his hand and ask questions if he does not understand what the teacher said or what he read. As mentioned earlier, he has to advocate for his own learning. He has to take the responsibility to make sure he grasps the lesson. This is because he needs to build the foundation for further learning and because he will probably be tested on the material. If he cannot ask immediately, he should write down his question so he doesn't forget it, and then ask as soon after as possible.

Younger students tend to have very structured work that is often done by the class in a group, under the teacher's direction. For example, the teacher may lead a math lesson by telling the class to open their workbooks to page ten and take out a pencil. One child will then be called on to read the first problem while the teacher writes it on the board. The teacher will demonstrate how to solve the problem and will then call on someone to solve the next one while the rest of the class writes the numbers in their workbook. Older students are more likely to have to take notes when the teacher discusses history, explains math procedures, or analyzes literature. Notes should be brief, and include key words, not full sentences. The notes should capture main points with supporting examples. It is especially important that notes contain points that the student finds tricky to understand or is unlikely to remember on his own.

One of a student's jobs in class is to write down the homework assignment. If the teacher does not leave the assignment written on the board long enough to copy it, the student or parent should request that it be left up longer. At some schools, teachers also post their assignments on

the school's website or make a telephone record-
ing of the day's or week's assignments. Having
a reliable study buddy, a friend to call to get the
assignment if necessary, is an old standby.

At the end of the day, Junior needs to read
over his homework assignments to be sure he
packs the books, worksheets, or other materials
he will need to complete the assignments. Once
home, he needs to review his class notes. Review-
ing the notes reinforces Junior's understanding
of the material, prepares him for homework and
protects him in case of a pop quiz. Junior must
then review the workbook pages he completed
in class and triage his homework assignments by
priority.

Doing homework

Junior's first step in triage requires considering
which assignments are due the next day and which
are long-term assignments, due at the end of the
month. Next, he should organize assignments by
difficulty level and the time required to complete
them. Let's suppose that today third-grader Junior
was assigned to memorize three new spelling
words and calculate ten subtraction problems. He
also has to read Chapter Two in his storybook. All of
these assignments are due tomorrow. In addition,
Junior's teacher assigned the class a long-term
project of learning about a famous artist. In four
weeks, Junior will have to make an oral presentation about Van Gogh.

Junior is pretty good at spelling, but knows

he needs to take his time in arithmetic. He enjoys reading and the chapters of his book are short. He feels overwhelmed thinking about the Van Gogh project. Considering this, Junior decides to learn the spelling words first. He figures he can knock that off pretty quickly and it will give him a sense of accomplishment. Also, by studying the spelling words first, he can test himself again after he finishes each other portion of his homework to be sure he really memorized the correct spellings. Next, he'll do the arithmetic because it's hard and he won't be tired yet.

Junior sits down at his desk and takes out a pencil and paper. "The word is healthy" he says aloud. "H, E, A, L, T, H, Y." Junior writes the word "healthy" five times, stating the spelling aloud each time as he writes. "Kitchen" and "reference" are likewise written and recited aloud.

Feeling confident of his three new spelling words, Junior opens his math workbook to page fourteen and tackles his subtraction problems. Sometimes he needs to use his fingers or draw tally marks; sometimes he can figure it out in his head. Occasionally, he asks his mother if he is doing it right. Numbers with zero in them confuse him and he has to work on those problems extra slowly. Junior plans to ask Mrs. Robbins to explain again about subtracting numbers with zero in class on Tuesday. Finally, the page is done but Junior is not sure that all of his answers are right.

Having finished his arithmetic, Junior tests himself on his three spelling words. He correctly recites and spells each one.

Satisfied with his spelling, Junior happily pulls

out his storybook and reads Chapter Two. His joy at finishing his homework is short lived when he realizes he has to figure out what to do about Van Gogh. Mother asks Junior what he will have to tell the class in his presentation. The conversation might go something like this: "I have to talk about who Van Gogh was, when and where he lived, his most famous works, and why he's special," replies Junior checking his assignment sheet.

"That's four things," states Junior's mother.

"I have four weeks to do the work so I could do one part each week," Junior proposes.

Mother nods. "That's right, you can break it up into four pieces and do a little of each piece every day and then you'll be all done by the due date. Break the work into small pieces and write each piece on your daily planner to stay on track." Suddenly the long-term assignment doesn't seem so huge and overwhelming to Junior anymore.

"Do we have any pictures by Van Gogh?" Junior asks Mother.

"Yes, the *Starry Night* picture in the foyer is by Van Gogh. Of course it's just a copy, but it's still beautiful." Junior runs to the foyer, confident in his ability to complete the long-term project.

Although in this example Junior is presented as highly competent, students will in fact need parental instruction in these study skills as well as parental supervision and help to stay on track.

It takes time and practice to master and internalize these study skills, but they will benefit students throughout their educational years.

Junior's Homework Plan

At School:

1. Copy the homework assignment from the board.
2. Pack the relevant books and materials.

At Home:

3. Review class notes.
4. Organize homework into "due tomorrow" and "due later."
5. Divide "tomorrow" homework into "quick and easy" and "harder and needs more time."
6. Do the "quick and easy" homework for tomorrow.
7. Do "harder and needs more time" for tomorrow.
8. Prioritize "due later."
9. Do part of the "due later" assignment.
10. Put the homework in its folder and put the folder in the backpack.

While Junior counts all the colors in the Van Gogh picture, his older cousin Nick, a fifth grader, chips away at his homework. Nick must read a chapter in a social studies textbook and answer questions about Eskimos. "There's so much in this chapter. How am I ever going to learn this and answer the questions?" he sighs.

Nick needs to learn to read a textbook. He already knows how to read a storybook or novel—just start at the first page and keep going until you get to the last page. But reading a textbook is different. Nick is trying to find out information, not follow a storyline. Textbooks usually have quiz questions at the end of each chapter. Nick needs to start by reading the questions first. This will orient him to the information he needs to find. Today Nick needs to answer questions about Eskimo clothing and diet.

After reading the questions, Nick turns to the beginning of the chapter. Next, he reads all the section headings and finds the pages that discuss clothes and diet. He reads the page about diet, highlights key points (not everything!) and makes a notation in the margin when there is something he does not understand. (Note: If the textbooks belong to the school rather than to the student, he must take notes and write questions in a notebook, to keep the textbook clean.) When Nick finishes the section, he looks up the confusing vocabulary word in the glossary at the back of the textbook and re-reads the sentence it was in. Now it makes sense. Nick closes the book and recites *out loud* all the points he can remember from the section about Eskimo clothing. Then he opens the book to see if he remembered correctly and fully. Forcing himself to say the information aloud reveals whether Nick truly absorbed it. It is easy to cheat and fool yourself if you review the points mentally. By saying them aloud, Nick proves what he retained and what he did not. Nick re-reads any part that he did not recall correctly and repeats the procedure with the part about the Eskimo diet. Then he is able to write down the answers to the questions. Nick writes as neatly as he can, because he knows that neater work means a better mark.

Nick's little sister, Lisa, finds it hard to get started on her homework. It all seems so much. Lisa's babysitter helps her do it in manageable steps. She sets the kitchen timer for ten minutes and while it ticks, Lisa works. When the bell rings, the babysitter sets the timer for three minutes of recess when Lisa can get a drink, play with her cat or just close her eyes. When the bell rings, the babysitter sets the timer for another ten minutes of work. The cycle is repeated until Lisa finishes her homework. The kitchen timer method allows students to tackle their work in small increments instead of feeling as if they must climb a tall mountain. Since Lisa knows a break is coming, she feels less overwhelmed and is able to persevere and get her work done. The amount of work time and recess time can be adjusted for a student's age, grade, or personal needs.

When a student finishes all the homework that is due the next day, he must put the assignments in the appropriate folders and put the folders in his backpack. It is no use doing the homework and leaving it at home. Homework is not completely finished until it is packed up, ready to go to school.

Test taking skills

A test! Short of being sent to the principal's office, nothing strikes fear into a student's heart the way a looming test does. But a test need not be so frightening, especially when you know how to prepare for it. All tests are not alike.

Among the tests that students are likely to face are multiple choice tests, fill in the blank tests, short answer tests, essay tests, and oral tests. Each one makes its unique demands so it is helpful to find out in advance which style the test will be.

A multiple choice test presents a question with (typically) four answer choices. The student must select the answer choice that best responds to the question. In a fill in the blank test, the student is typically faced with sentences that have words missing. There is often a list or box of answer words at the top of the page from which the student must select for each sentence. In a short answer test, the student writes his or her own brief answer to each question. An essay test requires students to produce longer written answers, ranging from a few paragraphs to a few pages. For an oral assessment, the student must speak aloud his or her replies. This type of test is most likely to be given in a foreign language class.

Regardless of the style of test, it is crucial for students to read and understand the directions. I know teachers who make this point very clear by giving their class a test that asks students to do simple things such as draw a circle, add two plus two, and clap their hands. The directions, which many students do not read, state that the students should *read all the items before starting to work.* The last item tells students to ignore the test and read a book. It quickly becomes apparent who read and followed the directions and who did not. Some students have been known to write lovely essays that earned F's because they did not read the question carefully and thus responded to the wrong topic.

It has become a cliché to ignore directions whether building a bookcase or driving someplace. Nonetheless, paying attention to directions at the start of a task greatly facilitates its timely and accurate completion. Many teachers advise their students to read the directions and questions not just once but twice, to be sure of what is being asked.

If students are given an assignment that will prepare them for a test, they should do the assignment under test conditions. For example, if students will be required to write a two-page essay during one hour of class time, they should approach the homework essay as if it were the test. That means setting a timer for the allotted time and using only those notes or other materials that will be permitted during the actual test. On the actual test, students should try to write as neatly as they can. For a homework essay, after the draft is done, students should type or neatly re-write the copy that will be handed in to the teacher.

To study for a vocabulary test, study in both directions. That is, say the word and afterward say its definition. Then go in reverse; state a definition and afterward state the word. This system works for foreign language translations and chemistry formulas too. Students can make a set of flash cards. They will learn as they write their cards as well as when they practice with them.

When an upcoming test is announced, students should include test study time as part of their homework routine. The routine of studying class notes daily will facilitate test preparation. It is more effective to study for shorter, more frequent sessions than for a very long session just before the test. As you have probably heard before, the night before the test, students should go to sleep at a sensible time. They should eat a good breakfast in the morning, bring pencils, etc., and wear a watch.

As stated above, when taking a test, a student should start by reading the directions and underlining key words (e.g., *define, match, always, except, not, explain*). For a multiple-choice test, students should read the question and *all* of the answer choices even if they think the first one is correct. Sometimes there are surprises. If a student does not know an answer, and if there is no penalty for a wrong answer, he should guess. If points or partial points are subtracted for wrong answers, it may not be worth guessing unless the choice can be narrowed down to two. For matching questions where one must draw lines connecting information, watch where the lines are going. Using a ruler can be helpful here. There are vocabulary or fill in the blank sentence tests where the words to be used are listed in a box and the children select one or more per question. Many children have a habit of crossing out words after they use them, often covering them up completely. Tell Junior not to cross out words so that he cannot read them as he may realize a mistake and need to see the words in the choice box. For short answer tests, have Junior skip lines as he writes to allow room to edit. For essay tests, Junior needs to pick an appropriate topic and focus it narrowly enough. Junior then needs to brainstorm ideas and organize them, followed by writing a brief outline. Next, Junior will write the introduction, supporting arguments, and conclusion. Again, have Junior skip lines as he writes to allow room for editing at the end. Having a written outline may gain a student some points in case time is called before the essay is finished. The outline shows the teacher the student's line of thought.

When students get their tests back, they should seek clarification of anything that they got wrong. This is because they need to understand the material and because the issue could appear on a future test. Keep quizzes and tests in a folder to use as study materials for a final exam. But first post that great score on the fridge!

Coping with "going blank"

Many students have told me that sometimes they look at the test questions and feel as if their minds went blank. I had this experience a number of times myself as a student. It is a very uncomfortable feeling but it can be overcome.

The first step in dealing with a blank feeling is to study efficiently and steadily for the test. If a student has not studied, there is no getting over the blankness because he really does not know the material. The second step is for the student to take a few deep breaths and remind himself that he studied and that he can do this. The teacher gives tests based on the lessons studied. The student should read the question slowly and carefully, twice, even three times if need be. Slowing down to think carefully and determine what the question is asking for is a key part of answering correctly. This allows the student to make the connection between the question and the material covered in class, and quietly tell himself what to do.

I advise students not to look at their peers if they get nervous. If they see other children writing busily it can upset them further; also, they might be accused of cheating. There may, however, be information posted on the classroom walls that could help them answer the questions, and that is fair game to look at. If the teacher does not want students to see the posters, she should take them down or cover them up. Many students have told me that once they write their first answer they feel much calmer and more confident.

Utilize community resources

Students should avail themselves of community resources to supplement their textbooks and classroom instruction. As previously mentioned, homework help hotlines and websites can provide extra explanations and support. Students can learn a lot about a subject from websites, but should not limit themselves to the computer. They need to know how to access information in a library. School librarians teach classes how to do this and students can also learn this skill at a public library. Students need to know how to obtain information from primary sources (e.g., original historical document) and secondary sources (e.g., biography of a famous person). Librarians can teach students time saving skills in using computer search engines to obtain reliable, factual information. They can also recommend fiction books that provide a sense of background about a place or time period, even if the characters and story are made up.

Museums are another community resource offering scholastic support. In addition to traditional museums of paintings and sculpture, there are museums devoted to television and radio, clothing styles, science, how people lived in previous times, and even baseball. Given the enormous array of topics, there is bound to be an exhibition relevant to your son's curriculum. Accompany him on a guided tour and learn from the docent. Let Thomas try to copy a painting to see it from his own active angle. He can also stand in the posture of a sculpture to appreciate its grace or power. The museum may have children's classes where Thomas can experience using a potter's wheel or a hammer and chisel. Such experiences broaden a student's perspective and enhance his understanding and participation in class.

Another community resource is the theater. If students are reading a play in class, there is nothing like seeing it performed to really enjoy it. Likewise, if Lulu is learning to play Mozart on her cello, take her to a concert to hear his works. Try to sit with a good view of the cellists so she can watch their fingering and bowing.

Use vacation time constructively

My children's school district requires summer reading and math work and yours might also. Even if it does not, keep your children actively engaged in reading and math skills during the summer because students' skills regress somewhat over the summer without instruction. The assigned reading and math packets help to keep students' skills fresh so they can hit the ground running in the autumn with less time needed for review. When students hand in their summer work, it shows their commitment to learning. The packet work is often part of the September grade.

What should children read over the summer? Reading is reading no matter what the form. If your son enjoys sports, let him read the sports section of the newspaper. If your daughter enjoys fashion and movie stars, let her read popular magazines that cover these topics. Encourage the reading of books by doing it together. Take turns reading a chapter aloud. Your child may also be helped by listening to a book on tape while reading along in the text. Listen to books on tape in the car and discuss them as a family while traveling. Attend library story time with younger children. In all cases, discuss what your child reads to improve comprehension skills.

How can you help maintain math skills during vacation time? Encourage children to keep an estimated running total of items while shopping in the supermarket; see how close they come to the actual bill. Have your kids help measure ingredients when you cook. If they want to build a tree house or dog house, have them help with the angles, circumference, and other measuring tasks involved. Swimming races and other sports can include math by timing the children's speed and graphing progress over the summer.

Another way to use vacation time constructively is to enroll Juanita in a summer review course. If she struggled with reading comprehension, a summer class will keep her actively focused on improving her reading skills.   Juanita will feel better prepared when she starts her new grade in September.

A similar option is to take a "prep" class to prepare for a challenge in the upcoming school year. After my junior year of high school, I took a summer French class to prepare for an International Baccalaureate final exam that loomed at the end of my senior year.   Although I was a good French student, taking the course boosted my confidence along with my skills, which made the IB less scary. The summer course was not available through my school; my family had to find it elsewhere. My daughter, Sandra, had the opportunity to be jumped a level in math in middle school. She wanted to take on this challenge and worked with a summer tutor to prepare her for the qualifying exam.

In her sophomore year of high school, my daughter, Kara, studied about life in the American colonies during the 1600's, and part of the curriculum included the notorious Salem witch trials. Our family spent a weekend in the Boston area and toured Salem. Seeing the actual houses with period furnishings where the accused witches had lived and the dreadful, frightening jails, made this period in history truly vivid, not only for Kara but for all of us. Visiting historical sites tied to your child's curriculum adds immeasurably to his or her understanding beyond the classroom.

While not possible for every family, travel to another country can be highly educational for students. It gives them a chance to practice the foreign language they have been learning, to experience the culture and typical foods first-hand, and to get a glimpse of real life in that country. Connections can be made with the school curriculum, religion, or family ancestry. Travel provides an *in vivo* experience of trying something new.

Despite all of the above ways to use vacation time constructively, a student also needs down time, which is not as non-constructive as it may seem. Sports and socializing are important as children need to develop physical and social skills too. School is work for children and they are entitled to some rest and refreshment in their time off.

Learning to manage time and resources in order to progress academically is a vital skill for students to develop. Parental assistance is important for children's growth in this area. Parents help children avail themselves of resources near and far, to practice study skills, and provide encouragement.

Key points from Chapter Six:

1. Students need to develop study skills in order to progress academically.
2. Study skills begin with self-advocacy in the classroom.
3. Students need to know how to triage homework, how to read a textbook, and how to organize their studying.
4. There are test studying techniques that students need to learn.
5. There are test taking techniques that students need to know.
6. Utilize community resources to enhance learning.
7. Use vacation time constructively to increase learning.

Questions for parents to pursue:

1. Does your child advocate for himself at school?
2. Can your son triage his homework appropriately?
3. Is your daughter able to work on projects step by step over time?
4. Does your child understand the differences among types of tests? Does he or she understand how to approach each type?
5. Is your son studying for tests in an effective manner?
6. Are you helping your child avail himself of supportive community resources (e.g., museums, concerts, public library)?
7. Do you look for educationally constructive things to do during vacation time (e.g., take extra classes, travel, visit historical sites)?

CHAPTER SEVEN

NON-SPECIAL EDUCATION SUPPORTS AVAILABLE IN SCHOOL

Exploring extra help

When a student needs extra academic help, the first step is to speak with his or her teacher to determine what types of support are available at the school, and what type of support is relevant for the student. If one teacher uses a technique that is helpful to your child, share it with his or her other teachers.

The first level of support is within the classroom. The teacher can call on Donald or Donna and ask him or her to repeat the instructions and explain them to the class. This gives the student an extra chance to review and process the information. It would be best if the teacher would call on two or three students to repeat this exercise, in order not to single out and embarrass the struggling learner. Giving a "heads up" to students can be helpful as well. "I'm going to call on Sima, Simon, and Serena in the next ten minutes," announces Mrs. Johnson. Alternatively, the teacher can say "In the next five minutes, I want the class to give me three examples of why the colonists resented British governance." The heads up increases focus and participation, allows time to prepare an answer, and gears up the students to ask questions if they are unclear about the material.

Similarly, a shy student like Mary can work a deal. Mrs. Johnson will ask the class a question. If Mary's hand is up, Mrs. Johnson will call on her. If Mary does not raise her hand, Mrs. Johnson or her teaching assistant will repeat the information and walk Mary through it. Having a teaching assistant in the room helps students review information and practice more examples. The assistant can also alert the teacher where the student's confusion appears to lie, so that the teacher can work on clarifying the point.

If a student needs more time to go over the curriculum, she could meet with the teacher before school, during lunch, or after school, depending on school policy. When Sally meets Mrs. Johnson for a "working lunch," she is likely to find Dick and Jane there, too. Realizing that she is not the only one who is confused will soothe Sally and encourage her learning. Some schools also have adult volunteers from the community available in the school to offer extra help. Peer mentors, who are often older students (e.g., high school students working with elementary students), may also be available to tutor students as part of a community service requirement from their church or an organization such as the National Honor Society. Struggling students may need to be referred to work with a volunteer by their teacher or parent, as per school rules.

In some schools, there is a homework club that meets after school. The club's meeting time is specifically for students to work on their homework in a quiet room such as the school's library. The homework club is supervised by teachers who are available to encourage and help students when they need it. Some students do not have a quiet place to work at home, or the demands of family life are such that having the student attend homework club is the best option for them to reliably complete their work. Doing the homework in a group provides structure, focus, and supports the sense of belonging to a community of learners. Homework club is open to all students, regardless of academic level, so it does not imply that the participants have any academic concerns.

Some public schools offer a "Saturday Academy," where students receive extra preparation for state mandated tests. This service is open to all of the students attending the school. Other schools or districts may or may not offer similar opportunities.

Managing test anxiety

Some students understand their classroom instruction and textbooks and perform satisfactorily on classroom work and homework assignments, but "go blank" when taking a test. Even though they studied and really did learn the material, they freeze when the test lands on their desks. As mentioned above, there are psychological techniques to help students cope with "test freeze."

Many students can get past the blank feeling by re-reading the question and taking a few deep breaths. They use positive self-talk; they say encouraging things to themselves, to remind themselves that they studied and really do know the material and can answer the question. Sometimes, students need to practice anxiety management techniques on a regular basis in order to stay calm during tests. One technique that many students have told me is helpful is to imagine that they are in a place that makes them happy, such as the beach. I guide them through visualizing the beach, "seeing" the waves and the sand and "hearing" the seagulls' cries. In their imagination, I have them "smell" the salty sea air and "taste" the hot dogs that are cooking on the grill. I ask the students to "feel" the rough dry sand and "squeeze" the squishy wet sand through their fingers. Slowly and peacefully imagining their favorite place and exploring it with all of their senses brings a calm, relaxed feeling that enables the students to regain confidence and focus for their academic work. When a student is proficient in using this relaxation technique, briefly conjuring up an image of the beach is often enough to help him feel peaceful and able to return to his test questions.

Students can be referred to the School Psychologist on an informal basis to learn such techniques. The students do not need to be "emotionally disturbed" or have a diagnosis to meet with the School Psychologist on an occasional basis. This can be arranged in consultation among the teacher, parent and psychologist. With the consent of the school administration, the psychologist could teach relaxation techniques to the entire class.

Federally financed supports for students

There are several federal programs that provide support to struggling learners to help them improve their academic functioning. These can be collectively referred to as "Title Programs." Title programs can be available in both public and private schools that receive federal funding. Nonetheless, a school district is not obliged to apply for and offer such support.

Title I (A) provides funds for the remedial educational support of at-risk or failing students in core subject areas. The funds can be used to hire remedial teachers, pay for supplies and equipment, offer training for staff or parents, and participate in BOCES (Board of Cooperative Education Services) or other programs that improve student achievement. Sheldon is a second grade student struggling to learn to read, who receives Title I (A) funded instruction in a small group. During reading time, his class breaks into small groups, as per reading level. Sheldon and three other children meet with their reading specialist teacher for intensive instruction that supports and parallels the instruction provided by the regular classroom teacher. Attendance in Title I instructional groups is arranged in consultation among the teacher, parent, and school administration.

Title II (A) provides for professional development of school staff. Teachers attend workshops, seminars, and educational conferences pertaining to their subject of instruction. The schools can also use the money to hire experts to teach the teachers, observe them in the classroom, and provide constructive feedback to enhance their performance. When teachers enhance their skills, students are likely to improve their learning.

Title II (D) provides federal money toward instructional technology to assist students with learning. Schools apply these funds toward integrating technology into the curriculum to boost student achievement. The funds can be used to buy computers, software, and multi-media equipment, as well as provide training to staff to further students' progress. Students enjoy using computers and teachers can use computer programs with appealing graphics to teach phonics, vocabulary, or math skills in engaging ways.

Title III (A) refers to the federal funding to support students who are learning English as a second language. The money can be used to pay for teaching materials and to hire staff and provide professional development training for them, all toward the goal of boosting students' command of the English language. It is quite a challenge for a foreign born child to learn English at school. Experts say it takes two to three years to develop competence in social English but five to seven years to develop academic competence. Despite this, in my personal experience as a student attending an international school, I observed that non-English speaking classmates were able to learn English successfully and with amazing rapidity. Many times, their parents were highly educated and spoke English, factors that facilitated the learning process for the children. Learning English as a second language is a greater challenge when one's parents do not speak English and have limited education in their native language as well. Nonetheless, it can be done as many students have proven to me.

Title IV pays for programs that support mental health and social-emotional well-being, and teach students about the dangers of using recreational drugs. Funds may be applied toward research-based programs or toward the hiring of counselors to provide on-site counseling services to students. Although Title IV is not specifically geared toward raising academic achievement, mental health and social-emotional issues or drug use may be behind academic difficulties for some students.

Title V covers innovative programs to support academic progress. Title V programs are not available in all districts or might be time-limited. Parents need to inquire whether Title V programs are available at their child's school.

It is important to note that some Title programs provide direct instruction to students, while others train staff to enhance their skills in working with students. Parents may consult with the school principal or the Director of Funded Programs in their district to determine which program may be relevant to their child. Parents may request that their child receive services under a Title program, but it is the school that determines the child's eligibility. The Director of Funded Programs may also be able to advise parents of free or low cost supportive programs available in the community.

Resource room services

Resource room is a special education service that can be available to regular education students on a time-limited and space-available basis when appropriate. This would be arranged in consultation with the child's teacher and the resource room teacher, based on the student's weak academic performance. In such a case, a student would be said to attend non-mandated resource room, even though he physically sits together with mandated children. When a student attends resource room, he meets with a special education teacher and a small group of students, to work on specific learning skills. The resource room teacher works on improving students' skills in specific areas (e.g., math reasoning), and targets specific underlying thought processes. The resource room instruction complements the regular classroom instruction but does not necessarily use the same lesson content. The resource room teacher and regular education teacher are in on-going consultation with each other.

Avery is an example of a student whose confidence and academic progress soared as a result of attending non-mandated resource room. This sweet, kind sixth grader had a history of being very shy, never wanting to speak in his regular classroom. In fact, some people thought he was growing prickly since he was reluctant to engage with them. During the course of the school year, Avery's confidence, social interaction skills (with peers and adults), and academic growth were substantial. He joked, he initiated conversations, and his language skills grew. Decoding, reading comprehension, vocabulary, and spelling all improved. In fact, his vocabulary and spelling improved so much that sometimes he bested teachers at the "hangman" word guessing game.

Attendance in non-mandated resource room can help the student in two ways. First, it helps increase academic skills. Second, if despite some gains, the student is not making expected progress, the attendance in non-mandated resource room might serve as an example of Response to Intervention. Should the parents decide to meet with the Committee on Special Education to determine whether their child requires special education, demonstration that "RTI" efforts were made will be required.

Public school mandated resource room and Title I are similar in that both provide academic support for struggling students. They differ in that Title I is not prescriptive, that is, students do not need formal testing to access it, whereas they must be tested and meet the state's definition of a handicapped student to be eligible for mandated resource room. (A student does not need to undergo testing for special education in order to access non-mandated resource room.) The Title I teacher helps students stay afloat in class; pre-review of the regular classroom material could be included, along with reviews of vocabulary and math facts. Resource room addresses areas of weakness and the underlying mental processes, but is not specifically linked to the lesson taught by the regular education teacher. Please note that a private school may offer its own resource room, separate from what may be available through a public school district, sometimes for an extra fee beyond the regular tuition. A private school's resource room may also differ from public school resource room regarding attendance time limits, teacher qualifications, amount of instructional time a student receives, or in other ways.

Non-mandated "related services"

Special education students are often referred to as "mandated students," because they are mandated by law to receive special education services, either a program (type of class) or a "related service" (e.g., speech therapy, occupational therapy). Related services support the student's functioning in his class. In some, but not all districts, certain related services (speech therapy, psychological counseling) can be available to regular education students as a support, on a limited basis, under certain circumstances. Sometimes this is referred to as "building level" service, in that it is provided in the school building, but not through the Committee on Special Education. If a parent is concerned that her child has a speech or language impairment, she should contact the Speech Therapist at her child's school to discuss the nature of the problem, its severity, and whether non-mandated speech therapy is appropriate for her child. For example, Nina has difficulty articulating a few sounds that a child her age should be able to say clearly. Nina's articulation trouble is mild and does not impinge on her learning, although it embarrasses her socially. She does well in class and uses language correctly, but can be hard to understand especially if she speaks rapidly. She meets with a Speech Therapist once a week to work on vocal exercises to improve her clarity, and is expected to practice at home with parental supervision.

Similarly, a student can have emotional or behavioral issues that are not severe enough to warrant special education services, but that nonetheless, interfere with appropriate educational or school functioning. I remember a fifth grade boy, Tyler, who was inclined to copy whatever misbehavior his peers committed. He was a satisfactory student but uncertain whether the other boys liked him, and reluctant to stand up for himself for fear they would exclude him. Tyler attended counseling on an informal, time-limited basis to work on his ability to express a difference of opinion from the group.

The school nurse can also be a source of support for students whose medical condition may hamper learning. Some students need to take medication during the school day or have their blood pressure checked periodically. Other students may be temporarily disabled (e.g., broken leg) and require nursing assistance during the school day. In-school vision screenings play a vital role in identifying students who need glasses so they can see the board properly. The school nurse also supports the entire student body by providing information to students about topics such as nutrition, exercise, cleanliness, vaccinations and general wellness.

Response to intervention

As mentioned above, Response to Intervention refers to constructive efforts to support an at-risk or failing student. RTI was part of the 2004 re-authorization of the Individuals with Disabilities Education Act and requires research-based methods, provided on a tier system to support struggling learners. Interventions need to be provided for a reasonable period of time and their success, or lack thereof, recorded. If a student is referred to the Committee on Special Education, it will be necessary to show that intervention efforts were made, but were not sufficient to support the student in general education. RTI is one of many pieces of data that the committee needs to review in order to determine whether the child requires special education to make appropriate academic progress.

Retention

Many parents worry that their child will be retained a grade due to insufficient academic progress. Retention, or repeating a grade, is one of a child's greatest nightmares due to the dual punch of intellectual and social disgrace. Many educators are of the opinion that retention does no good because it is too emotionally overwhelming and provides no academic support in and of itself. Research indicates that initial gains are not maintained in the long term and that comparably low performing peers who are promoted do better than the children who are retained. Some recent findings are more hopeful regarding retained students' academic performance and self-confidence, but too new to be sure of long term impact.

If a child is to repeat a grade, and nothing is going to be done differently, why should the outcome be different? Will simply another round of exposure to the material enable Junior to understand it? It seems that if retention is to be done, there ought to be more support, there must be some difference in the way the student is taught in order to make the year more productive. Likewise, it would seem that there ought to be some difference even if the child is promoted. One parent told a colleague of mine, "why should my son stay in school an extra year; it's just going to prolong his suffering. Promote him and give him support."

Sometimes the decision to retain is educationally appropriate and there are test questionnaires to help school staff make the decision. Reasons favoring retention may include a child's frequent absences from school, frequent moves and changes of school, or medical issues that took time away from learning. Social immaturity is also a consideration, especially for younger children. If a child is to be retained, it is best to do it at a young age, kindergarten at the latest. One of my daughters had a pre-school classmate whose mother decided to retain her another year in pre-school. The little girl was socially and developmentally immature and did stand out from her peers. When I later saw her at a Girl Scout event, I saw a properly functioning, happy second grade girl. The mother's decision was correct in this case. Consider that it is only one year out of an entire lifespan. Besides, by being older than her or his classmates, a retained student will have the status of being the first one in the class to have a Bat or Bar Mitzvah, get a driver's license, host a Quince Años party, or achieve other social milestones.

If a student must be retained at a higher grade, not only must academic support be established, but consideration should be given to a change of school. The student may make a better social adjustment if his new friends do not know he is repeating a grade. Tho parents may also have concerns regarding the original school's ability to educate and support their child.

504 Plans

A 504 Plan provides accommodations to regular education students who have an impairment and a substantial limitation of a major life activity. Section 504 of the Rehabilitation Act of 1973 (Public Law 93-112) is federal legislation designed to prevent employment discrimination against people with disabilities, who are otherwise qualified for the job. In 1974, the act was amended to protect disabled students who attend or want to attend schools that receive federal funds. A 504 Plan is a separate entity from an IEP (Individual Education Program, the document that states the special education services a classified student receives) and does not classify a student as eligible to receive special education services. Rather, it provides accom-modations to enable a student to pursue his or her education in a regular education program.

A team of school staff members writes the plan in cooperation with the student's parent.

In order to qualify for a 504 Plan, a student must have a documented physical or mental impairment *and* the impairment must result in a "substantial limitation of a major life activity." Major life activities include but are not limited to: breathing, eating, self-care, seeing, walking, and learning. Such a student may receive reasonable and appropriate accommodations to enable him or her to pursue an education. To give some examples, a student with vision deficits may require a large print textbook. With such a textbook, he may read the lesson just as anyone else in his class does. A student with allergies to chalk dust would need to be taught in a room where a dry erase board is used in place of a chalkboard. Marcus is a middle school student with an orthopedic impairment whose 504 Plan grants extra passing time in the hallway between classes. Students with Attention Deficit Disorder may require extra time on tests and that the test is taken in a room with minimal distractions. There are many possible accommodations, based on the student's individual needs.

There is no legal definition of "substantial limitation" and school districts may define it as they see fit. However, it must be emphasized that the presence of a disability is not sufficient; there must be a substantial limitation of a major life activity. I recall a student diagnosed with ADD who nonetheless had a grade point average of 90; this student was not substantially limited in his learning. The purpose of a 504 Plan is to "level the playing field," to enable a child to participate in his education. It is not intended to raise grades. Once the student with vision deficits can read his assignment in a large print textbook, it is up to him whether he answers questions correctly or incorrectly. A 504 Plan is a legal document with its own eligibility requirements. That a parent or teacher thinks the child "could do better" is not the issue. A 504 Plan is not "special ed lite" and is not an end run around special education. It is not a consolation prize for students who do not qualify for special education services.

Rona was a slender, fifth grade girl who was well behaved and worked hard but struggled mightily with mathematics. Her family discussed her situation with the Committee on Special Education (CSE) where it was determined that she did not meet the state's criteria to be classified as a special education student. Nonetheless, the record showed that she had a significant processing disorder and a long history of challenge in learning mathematics; her performance in other subject areas was within expectations for a student of her IQ level. Accordingly, she received a 504 Plan to provide accommodations in math. Accommodations included preferential seating, a copy of the class notes, extra time on tests, tests taken in a location with minimal distractions, and that the test directions should be explained. Rona still found math challenging but the accommodations helped her to perform satisfactorily and receive a passing grade in the course.

The provisions of a 504 Plan need to be implemented consistently. If a child requires extra time on tests, that means all tests, not just the big ones.

If a child is not using his accommodations and is achieving passing grades, there is reason to believe he no longer requires the plan. Section 504 Plans must be reviewed "periodically." While a three-year cycle is permissible (similar to IDEA's triennial re-evaluations for special education students), it is better practice to review the plan each year to be sure it is still required and that the specific accommodations chosen are appropriate for the child's current needs.

It is important that the parents (and students who are old enough) confirm that the teacher is aware of the 504 Plan. Your child will have a new teacher each year and some teachers may not have had first-hand experience with 504 Plans, even though they are aware of them in theory. The parents need to advocate on behalf of their child and make sure that the 504 Plan is being implemented appropriately and consistently. The School Psychologist is available to provide consultation and assistance to the teacher in implementing a 504 Plan's accommodations.

It should be noted that not all students denied special education services are eligible for a 504 Plan. Likewise, neither are all students who apply for a 504 Plan without applying to the Committee on Special Education eligible either. The parents of a sixth grade boy wanted to obtain a 504 Plan because of a weak muscle in his hand. At a meeting with the parents and the boy's teachers, each of the core subject teachers recommended the student for the honors program the following year. The parents asked "what about the 504?" School staff explained that although there was a documented physical impairment, no evidence was shown regarding substantial limitation in a major life activity. Every teacher recommended the boy for the honors program. Clearly, he was academically successful. The boy did not meet eligibility criteria for a 504 Plan. Just because a student has some kind of weakness, does not automatically mean that he or she is eligible for a 504 Plan. Each case needs to be considered individually. There are many situations where the full burden of providing academic support rests with the parents.

Parents like 504 plans for children with mild academic issues because they provide some support without the special education label. Ellen is a very bright twelve–year–old girl with one impaired ear who gets good marks but struggles to pass math. Her test scores and school performance indicate that she is an academically adequate student; therefore she is not eligible for special education. Ellen earns mostly decent marks because she works very hard, but nonetheless is challenged to hear instruction accurately. Due to the impact of her medical diagnosis on the major life activity of hearing, and the challenge it presents to her learning, she is eligible for a 504 Plan, a situation that satisfies her parents because they want Ellen to perform satisfactorily but they do not want her to be labeled as a special education student.

However, it must be noted that the level of academic support provided under a 504 Plan is typically less than what a student would get if she were classified to receive special education services. Ellen's 504 Plan provides accommodations such as a room with minimal noise in which to take tests and repetition of test directions. It does not address hearing per se. Ellen's parents have to consult their physician and their insurance company, and make their own arrangements for aids or other medical treatment to improve her hearing.

Principals like 504 Plans because the student remains in regular education and may do better as a result of the accommodations. Possible improvement may also be seen on state mandated tests, making the school's test scores look better.

There is no funding for 504 Plans as there is for special education. Although administering 504 Plans incurs some costs, they are less costly than special education.

There is a lot of help available to struggling students that does not involve special education. Students may attend extra help sessions with their teachers, obtain intensive instruction via Title programs, and work with specialists such as speech therapists and resource room teachers on a non-mandated basis. Certain needs may be accommodated through a 504 Plan. There are many options for regular education students to get help that comes under the umbrella of intervention. Parents should not hesitate to discuss their child's eligibility for non-mandated extra help with school staff.

Key points from Chapter Seven:

1. There are many options for helping regular education students.
2. A struggling student should start by contacting his teacher for extra help.
3. Tutors, peer mentors, and homework clubs are often available.
4. Title programs are offered to support struggling students.
5. Students may be able to work with specialist staff on a non-mandated basis.
6. Retention is a serious decision for parents to discuss with school staff.
7. Efforts to help students are "interventions." The student's "response to intervention" is an important part of helping him and of a referral to special education should that be considered later.
8. Some regular education students may be eligible for a 504 Plan providing accommodations in school.

Questions for parents to pursue:

1. Have you spoken to your child's teacher about extra help?
2. Find out what types of extra help programs are available at your child's school.
3. If the principal raises the question of retention, discuss the issue in depth before making a decision.
4. If you believe your child may be eligible for a 504 Plan, contact the School Psychologist.
5. Keep a log of the interventions your child receives, including the dates of service, the provider, and the content of the lessons.

CHAPTER EIGHT

PURSUING SPECIAL EDUCATION

Consult with the teacher and School Psychologist

If your child's learning problem persists despite sincere, on-going efforts to provide support at home and in school, it may be time to consider whether special education services are needed. Your first step is to have a meeting with your child's teacher and the School Psychologist where you can review your child's academic performance and his or her response to interventions, as well as gain a better understanding of special education services and procedures.

Review your child's report card, test grades, and homework assignments. Is Junior getting D's or F's, or does he have a C average when you were hoping for A's and B's? A C average is passing and therefore satisfactory. Consider your expectations of special education. Special education is not going to turn Junior into an honors student. That is not special education's function. Special education helps a student progress through his curriculum at a satisfactory level. Likewise, special education does not release you from parental responsibilities. Special education does not replace and cannot compensate for medical or therapeutic needs that are not being provided. Furthermore, special education cannot replace or compensate for the absence of other family-based responsibilities discussed in previous chapters. If you decide that your child's academic situation is not satisfactory and that he or she may require special education services in order to progress academically, it is time to learn the facts about eligibility for special education services, and what it means to have a classified child.

Learn about special education

Schedule a meeting with the School Psychologist to discuss your concerns. Either before or shortly after the meeting, you should read about your legal rights as parents regarding special education. The psychologist can provide you with a copy of this document. During the meeting, the psychologist will explain the details of applying to the Committee on Special Education (CSE). You should ask questions, and share your concerns. Express any fear or worry you might have; there are no stupid questions.

If you were meeting with me, I would start by listening to your concerns and clarifying what was previously tried to help your child, whether at home, in the community, or in school. I would ask about your child's social (developmental) history. Was your pregnancy routine or eventful in anyway? Was Junior's birth weight within normal limits, was he premature? What was he like as a toddler? What was his medical history? Many ear infections? Concussion, high fevers, seizures? Allergies? The school district asks for this information because it may impact on a child's ability to learn. For example, a child who has a history of frequent ear infections may have compromised hearing. Concussion or seizures may have caused neurological problems that interfere with consolidating information in memory. In addition to the social history, we would look at your child's academic record. What are Junior's strengths, what are his weaknesses? Are the difficulties recent or long-standing? We would discuss what academic interventions your child received and how he responded to them.

The school district requires your written consent to evaluate your child pursuant to an application to the CSE. Evaluation consists of psychological testing (IQ, visual-motor, personality, and other tests as relevant), educational testing (decoding, reading comprehension, spelling, writing, numerical reasoning, numerical operations, listening and oral skills), and if relevant, a speech and language evaluation, occupational therapy evaluation or a physical therapy evaluation. I will conduct the psychological evaluation. I will also observe Junior in the classroom and his teacher(s) will fill out one or more questionnaires about his academic and behavioral functioning. The teacher or a school administrator will provide copies of Junior's class work, latest report card, standardized test results, and any other pertinent information (e.g., detention record). You will have to submit the results of a recent physical examination by Junior's doctor to rule out medical reasons for difficulty at school.

If Junior attends a private school, you will have to register him in the relevant public school district.

This will be the district within whose boundaries the private school is located, which may or may not be the same district covering your residence. If it is not the same district, you may have to register him in your home district too. Registration means you must come to the district office with Junior's birth certificate, proof of your residency in the district, proof of Junior's immunizations, and other documents as required. Registration must be completed before public school staff may evaluate the child. If there are special circumstances (e.g., divorce, guardianship), you will be required to provide appropriate documentation as to your legal right to make school related decisions for Junior, regardless of whether he attends public or private school. You are welcome to submit reports from private practitioners who may have recently tested Junior or from other people who know him well and can provide relevant information. It takes some time to complete all the paperwork required for the meeting, although there is a legal timeline governing the process. If at any time during the process you decide that you wish to withdraw, you may do so, in writing. However, withdrawing will not address Junior's learning deficits.

Please bear in mind that different districts may follow procedures that vary somewhat from the above.

Your child's feelings about testing

Your child will be excused from class to be evaluated so he will miss some instruction. He may or may not be cooperative with the testing. A classmate might ask him why he was absent from class. An older student may resist the idea of receiving special education services. It is important to consider your child's feelings, especially if he is old enough to be consulted.

Many children I have tested thoroughly enjoyed the experience. I know this because they eagerly asked if I would be picking them up for more testing. They liked the puzzles, verbal challenges, and drawing subtests. You could see they were fully engaged in the tasks. Despite my best efforts at building rapport, there were also some children who resented being tested. They were uncomfortable missing class or worried about why they were being tested. Some knew their parents were considering a special education program and were upset and anxious about their responses to test questions. While some children conversed enthusiastically with me, others refused to speak beyond the minimum necessary. All styles of responses reveal information about the student but ideally the student should be calm, cooperative, and interested in doing his or her best. You need to consider carefully how you will inform your child about the impending testing. The psychologist can help you to prepare your child.

The CSE meeting

As Junior's parent, you need to prepare for and attend the CSE meeting. To prepare for the meeting, you need to read all of the evaluation reports and should discuss them with the staff that wrote them. It is vital that you understand everything in the reports because the test results will form a significant portion of the committee's decision. You must provide any document that it is your responsibility to provide (e.g., medical form from your physician) in a timely manner, as the meeting will not be held if the paperwork is not complete. In the district where I work, the parent must attend the meeting, as nothing will be done in an initial case without the parent being present. It is possible that other districts may have different practices, but it is in your child's best interest for you to be present at the meeting, even if your district does not require it.

If you have reason to believe that your child may be placed in a special education class, you should inquire about visiting such a class before the meeting, so that you will be in a better position to understand the recommendation and ask questions.

Parents who require a translator, a handicapped accessible meeting room, or who have some other special need, should inform school staff of same when they request evaluations.

Parents typically ask me two questions: what will happen at the meeting and what kind of services will Junior get. I can address the first easily, but cannot give a definite answer to the second. The decision regarding services is a decision to be made by the committee as a whole, during the meeting. You will get a letter inviting you to your child's meeting. In attendance along with you, the parent, will be a chairperson, psychologist, regular education teacher, special education teacher, parent member, and if relevant a related service specialist, such as a speech therapist, occupational therapist or physical therapist. New York State, where I work, requires that a "parent member" serve on the committee. The parent member is not the parent of the child under discussion; that adult is the parent. A parent member is a parent of a child who has been through the process and whose child receives special education services. The parent member, a volunteer, is there to "hold the hand" of the parent, provide parent to parent advice about helping children learn, and reassure parents, some of whom are anxious about the meeting. As the parent, you have the option to request in writing that the meeting be held without a parent member. You may also bring a relative, friend or other advisor to the meeting. Attendance rules may vary in different places.

At the meeting, you will be asked to share your concerns about your child. Why do you believe your child requires special education services? What have you done at home to assist your child? What has been your experience working with your child's school? The various professionals will discuss the findings from their evaluations of Junior and will share their experiences of working with him in school. The teacher will describe Junior's day–to–day functioning in class. When all of the information has been presented, the committee, which includes you, the parent, will make a determination whether Junior meets the criteria of a student with an educational handicap. If so, the chairperson will clarify the child's "handicapping condition," which refers to the reason Junior is eligible. This is what parents call "the label." Handicapping conditions include learning disability, speech impairment, mental retardation, hearing impairment and emotional disability, to name just a few. The average parent hears "handicapped" and thinks "wheelchair," but the term is very broad and refers to numerous types of weakness. The number of handicapping conditions and their specific titles or definitions may vary across states. Once it is determined that the child meets the criteria of a student with a handicapping condition, the committee will discuss what program or services would be appropriate to support his learning (e.g., resource room, self-contained class, speech therapy).

At this point if you sign a written consent, arrangements will be made to provide the special education services as soon as possible, within the legal timeline. The services will be in effect for one school year. Toward the end of the school year (or in some places, on the anniversary of the child's classification, or some other scheduling arrangement) you will be invited to another meeting to review your child's progress and determine his or her needs for the following year. If you refuse consent for special education services, no service will be provided. If you disagree with the committee's decision, because you believe different or more special education services are appropriate, there is an appeals process. If you choose not to give consent, you may prefer to obtain appropriate services privately at your own expense outside of school. In such a case, the school district is not involved in or responsible for the arrangements. You should ask about anything that is not clear because you are participating in an important decision for your child.

If your child is classified

Following the CSE meeting, an IEP (Individual Education Program) will be printed and mailed to you. This legal document states your child's classification, special education program and related services. It also summarizes the committee's rationale in deciding your child's eligibility and lists the goals to be addressed by special education staff members during the school year. The IEP typically runs several pages. You should read the IEP and ask if anything is not clear. School staff members who work with your child have the right to read it so that they can provide the services; otherwise it is confidential and cannot be released without your written consent.

You should note the date that services are scheduled to start and contact the special education staff members involved to introduce yourself and ask how you can support their work at home. Students who receive special education services receive annual testing to measure their progress. Every three years, the student will receive triennial testing, a full battery of tests similar to the initial testing, to further understand his or her progress and clarify his or her educational needs.

As mentioned above, there will be an annual review meeting in the spring (or at some other designated time, depending on your district's practices), when you will meet with your child's regular and special education teachers to confirm his program for the following year. If you have concerns during the school year and want to make a change in your child's IEP, you may request a meeting with the CSE at any time to discuss this. You should be prepared to present some documentation to support making the change you wish in your child's program.

In the event that you move out of district or out of state, you need to provide the new school district with a copy of your child's IEP to request special education services at his new school. The new district will likely honor the IEP for a limited time and schedule a meeting with you to determine if your child meets eligibility under their criteria. All districts or states are not alike. A child may qualify for some special education services in one but not the other. Regardless of where you live, there will be procedures to support your child and you need to continue supportive action at home.

If your child is ineligible for special education services

Not every problem can be addressed by a state or school district. There are many children whose weaknesses fall into a gray area. There is a weakness, but it does not rise to the level of meeting the state's definition of a handicapped student. In such cases, the committee will declare the student ineligible for special education services. Sometimes the student may qualify for a 504 Plan as discussed above. In many cases, the student does not qualify for any service. Parents then need to decide if they wish to obtain private support at their own expense. Not every family can afford this path, but the community may have places that offer help without charge or on a sliding scale basis. Parents may wish to consult with the school principal, school-community liaison, or Director of Funded Programs to see what arrangements might be possible going forward.

Special education has regulations, procedures, and criteria of eligibility of which parents should be aware. Parents need to have an in-depth discussion with the school psychologist to decide whether the pursuit of special education services is right for their child. The child will be tested and the process will follow a legal timeline. In pursuing special education parents have responsibilities, and will continue to have them after their child is classified or declared ineligible. Special education services can accomplish a lot to support children's learning but cannot address all situations. There are children who have academic weaknesses but not at the level of meeting the legal definition of a handicapped student. Regardless of the outcome of the CSE meeting, the results are not written in stone and the door is not closed. Parents may request a meeting with the CSE at any time to discuss their concerns regarding their child's special education program. If the child is declared ineligible, parents may request a meeting with the CSE at a future date if they have new information to present. As the parent, you monitor your child's progress and advocate on his or her behalf as needed.

Key points from Chapter Eight:

1. Despite serious, on-going efforts to support the child at school and at home, the child may not be making satisfactory progress.
2. Parents should have a serious discussion with the school psychologist to discuss whether special education might be appropriate for their child.
3. Parents need to fully understand the special education procedures, eligibility criteria, their rights and their responsibilities.
4. Parents need to prepare for and participate in the CSE meeting.
5. It is important to understand the special education services recommended.
6. There are many children who have weaknesses that do not result in eligibility for special education services.
7. Parents may need to follow private avenues of support if their child is not eligible for special education services.
8. Parents need to monitor their child's progress and advocate as needed.

Questions for parents to pursue:

1. How is my child doing? Discuss with teacher and psychologist.
2. Have I fully discussed special education procedures and issues with the psychologist?
3. Do I want to have my child evaluated for special education?
4. Do I understand the evaluation reports?
5. Do I understand how CSE meetings are conducted?
6. Am I clear about my rights and responsibilities if my child is classified?
7. What will I do for my child if he is ineligible for special education services?

CONCLUDING REMARKS

You've come a long way

You have come a long way since you first began reading this book. You may have started as worried, fearful, helpless, and embarrassed, but now are more confident, encouraged, positive, hopeful, and strengthened. You know you are not alone. Best of all, you have seen your Junior make academic progress.

Junior is feeling better, too. He learned to organize himself, which gives him the ability to acquire other vital skills. He learned study skills for both in the classroom and at home. He learned test taking skills. He learned how to calm himself down if he gets nervous. Junior is advocating for himself at school. He reaches out to learning opportunities around him in school, the community, and at home. He is re-vitalized in his eagerness and willingness to make an effort. He sees his efforts yield results and nothing can top that. School is again a positive place for him.

The key points

Parents can make a significant difference in their child's academic progress. Parents have so much to offer in the way of providing an organized home life for their child, a suitable place to study, the necessary study materials, and the respect for educational achievement.

When the importance of academic success

is clear, students rise to the occasion. Parents provide support through nutritious foods, medical and therapeutic care, and teaching all family members respect for academics. As much as possible, parents seek assistance from community resources, such as museums, libraries, historical sites, tutoring services, and homework help websites. They investigate the supports available in school to assist their child, such as extra help with teachers, Title programs, and non-mandated specialist services. Parents go the extra mile. They leave no academic stone unturned.

Parents demonstrate problem solving skills to their children when they partner with the teacher to address issues of concern. Sometimes, when a teacher expresses concern about a student's academic functioning, parents refuse to hear anything negative about their child and assume an adversarial stance. Perhaps you have been or were once tempted to be one such parent. You teach your child a valuable life lesson in cooperative problem solving by working together with the teacher and your child to develop a constructive plan of action. Such an approach helps your child learn to help himself to surmount obstacles.

The strong example set by the parents encourages the child to strive to advocate for himself. The child is a necessary part of his own success. He must ask questions, must learn appropriate study skills, and must understand how to approach tests. The most vigorous parents cannot compensate for a child who does not actively help himself learn. Student and parents must work as a team for the student to function satisfactorily in school.

They need to keep working as a united team in an on-going program; a one-time effort cannot produce the desired results. All team members need to encourage one another.

You are not alone. Your child's school staff members are there to assist you, not just during a specific episode, but also in an on-going capacity. Likewise, staff members delight in your child's progress and enjoy cheering him on alongside of you. Learning continues throughout life in one form or another. There are always challenges of one type or another. With the joint support of teachers and parents, your child will be secure in the knowledge that he or she is capable of successfully negotiating whatever challenges life presents. I wish you and your child the best of luck.

REFERENCE LIST

Diament, M. (2009, April 23). Poor Graduation
     Rates, Racial Disparities Persist In NYC
     Special Ed., Report Says. *Disability Scoop.*
     Retrieved from
     http://www.disabilityscoop.com

Gordon, T. (1989). *Teaching Children Self-
     Discipline.* New York: Times Books.

Gustafson, C. (2009, March, 6). Program Helps
     Parents with Reading Skills. *Greenwich
     Time,* pp. A1, A4.

Medina, J. (2009, October 16). Students Held
     Back Did Better. *The New York Times*,
     p. A22.

Saulny, S. (2005, June 3). Study on Special
     Education Finds Low Graduation Rate. *The
     New York Times.* Retrieved from
     http://nytimes.com

Schemo, D. J. & Medina, J. (2007, October 27).
     Disabilities Fight Grows as Taxes Pay
     For Tuition. *The New York Times (National),*
     pp. A1, A14.

Smith, T. E. C. & Patton, J. R. (1998). *Section 504
     and Public Schools.* Austin, TX: Pro-ed.

WEBSITES

http://idea.ed.gov

http://www.ed.gov

http://www.iteachilearn.com

http://www.nces.ed.gov

About the Author

Ann Core Greenberg, Ph.D. is a licensed Clinical Psychologist and a certified School Psychologist. She earned her Bachelor's degree at Cornell University, her Masters and Doctorate at Long Island University. In a career spanning over twenty-five years, Dr. Greenberg has enjoyed many professional paths including working in hospital and clinic settings, teaching college and parenting courses, private practice, and working in schools with students from nursery to high school. Currently, Dr. Greenberg works for a large school district in Rockland County, New York, where the student body is highly diverse regarding national and cultural background, mother tongue, religion, race, and socio-economic level. Dr. Greenberg has published nine articles pertaining to subliminal activation, social awareness, health, and parenting. This is her first full length book. Dr. Greenberg resides in Greenwich, Connecticut with her husband and two scholastically successful daughters.